A Man Who Told Us the Truth

D1453094

A Man Who Told Us the Truth

...

Will Davis Jr.

ISBN: 0692566562
ISBN 13: 9780692566565

Library of Congress Control Number: 2015918094
Sangre de Cristo, Austin, TX

Additional Books by Will Davis Jr.

• • •

Pray Big
Pray Big for Your Marriage
Pray Big for Your Child
Pray Big for Your Life
Why Faith Makes Sense
Ten Things Jesus Never Said
Enough: Finding More by Living with Less
Wake-Up Calls: 101 Devotions for Sleepy Christians

To seekers of purpose, meaning and truth...

Contents

Can We Finish This Together?

• • •

I MET LAUREL IN THE Trough on the west side of Longs Peak. Longs is the northern-most, fourteen-thousand-foot mountain in Colorado and is considered one of the toughest climbs in the state.

The Trough consists of a nine-hundred-foot ascent up a steep gorge typically filled with loose rocks, ice and snow. For every two steps up you take, you feel as if you're slipping back three. One serious misstep could kill you. Climbers on Longs must navigate their way through the Trough after hiking over seven miles and gaining nearly a mile vertically. The Trough looks like it was designed by the mountain to create a true heartbreak moment for summit seekers. More than a few weary climbers have had their spirits broken and have chosen to turn back in this brutal section of the climb. I think it would fit well into any medieval painting of Hell.

That's where I found Laurel. She was a twentysomething, former US marine, who had been surprised by the difficulty of the climb. When I stumbled upon her, she was sitting in a very defeated posture with her head between her knees, having just vomited onto the rocks at her feet. Tears were streaming down her face. She was beaten—the mountain had claimed yet another victim.

I sat down next to Laurel, introduced myself and offered her some water. Then I started talking to her about the climb. I had been up Longs several times before. I recognized that look in Laurel's eyes and had experienced the very pain that she was feeling. But I also knew how close she was to the top. I knew that, perhaps with some better pacing, Laurel could reach the summit. And when she did, the hike would turn into one of the greatest experiences of her life.

So after talking a while and giving Laurel a chance to regain her composure, I offered to help her reach the top. I simply said, "Can we finish this together?" I promised to go slow, to stop frequently and to not laugh at her when she pouted, cried or just wanted to quit. And just over an hour later, Laurel reached the summit of that mountain. She cried tears of joy, hugged me and swaggered over to sign the summit journal. It was a great moment for both of us, but the payoff was all Laurel's.

I'd like to suggest that this book plays a similar role to the one I played with Laurel on the mountain. Trying to discover where ultimate truth really begins and ends—if it even exists—can be brutal work. It can leave you feeling very much like Laurel did on the mountain—worn out, sick and ready to quit. The difficulty of a genuine spiritual pursuit only increases when you have to filter through all the mixed messages you get along the way. Sometimes it's just helpful to have someone pull alongside and offer to help.

As you engage in your spiritual search, I can't lead you to a certain set of beliefs or convince you that my faith is the route you should choose. But I can share from my own experiences and struggles, as well as from those who I've been privileged to know and travel with along the way. I can show you the summit of belief that I have found, tell you how I got there and even show you how to get there as well.

But whether or not you choose to believe is your call. It should be.

WHICH WAY IS UP?

This book is about seeking ultimate summits. It wrestles with questions of truth and spiritual realities.

I am amazed at the number of people I meet who find themselves actually surprised by their own level of spiritual curiosity. Their reasons are varied, but the need for the search is nonetheless the same.

There's the woman who just went through a painful divorce, and she's wondering if she can ever trust and love again. There's the Fabio look-alike who does construction for a living. Women are lined up to get an evening with this guy, and yet he's spending most of his time these days thinking about the possible reality of God. There's the successful trial lawyer, a self-described "recovering Catholic," who is having strange urges to give church another try. There's the CEO who is coming to the terrifying realization that his money and expensive toys aren't enough. He's still hungry for more, something...spiritual. There's the irreligious parent who is just trying to stay one step ahead of her child's questions about God. There's the husband and father who has experienced yet another massive moral failure. He's beginning to wonder if he might not need some outside, spiritual input. There's the bright, highly educated, scientifically minded grad student. She has for years found evolution to offer satisfactory explanations for her existence. Now, however, she's finding that some of her previously accepted theories don't really answer life's more pressing questions. And there are the grieving husband and wife, whose sudden and tragic loss of their child has left them emotionally breathless. As mad as they are at God, they have found themselves looking for him, hoping to find some sort of meaning in their child's apparently senseless death. Each of these real people is a summit seeker.

Can you relate to any of them? Are you somehow a reluctant but still determined seeker? Are you surprised that you're reading a book about spiritual matters? Well, don't be too concerned about your lack of intelligence or some inherent weakness on your part. To be spiritual is actually quite normal. We are instinctively a spiritually inclined people. We seem to find it most natural to believe in something. There's probably good reason for that. There is the very great possibility that someone exists beyond you who is in fact wooing you.

A WILD PROPOSITION

In light of that possibility, I'd like to offer you a rather wild proposition. Now, given that we live in a culture that claims life is some big accident or that we were actually brought to earth by aliens, I don't feel so bad asking you to consider a claim that seems on the surface to be rather outrageous. So here it goes: I'd like you to consider the possibility that the answers to our most pressing questions can be found in the life, teachings and, strangely enough, the death of one man who lived over two thousand years ago. I'm inviting you to at least consider the possibility that Jesus of Nazareth, the humble Jewish carpenter and unlikely founder of the Christian faith, may indeed have been on to something when he said he was God's Son.

So, I'm asking you if, like Laurel, we can finish this together. I'm asking for permission to dialogue with you about the person of Jesus.

If your answer is yes, then turn to the next page and let's get going. The summit is waiting.

CHAPTER 1

Let's Talk about Truth

• • •

Truth (noun): 1. the state of being the case; 2. the body
of real things, events, and facts; 3. a transcendent,
fundamental, or spiritual reality; 4. a judgment,
proposition, or idea that is true or accepted as true.

—*WEBSTER'S ONLINE DICTIONARY.*[1]

THEY SIT CASUALLY AROUND TWO hastily pushed together coffee tables. Before them are an assortment of drinks—beer, coffee, bottled water, tea—and snacks. The group consists of four men, three Anglo and one African American, and two females, both Anglo. In the center of the group, with his hands gently clasped together in the classic church-steeple style, is a man who appears to be of Indian descent. He is speaking and clearly has the rest of the group's undivided attention.

These conversationalists are part of a worldwide phenomenon known as the Socrates Café. Inspired by its namesake's passion for life examination, Socrates Cafés are groups of adults who meet for a few hours a week to exchange ideas. There are no real rules or regulations in the groups: just bring your ideas and your open mind.

Currently, there are over six hundred regularly meeting groups around the world. They also have formed in prisons, airport terminals, nursing homes and even homeless shelters.

Christopher Phillips, the founder of the Socrates Café, is a lecturer, educator, writer and speaker who travels the world, encouraging the exchange of ideas according to the Socratic method. Phillips, who has written two books about the Socrates Café movement, has an interesting goal for the cafés: "The whole idea is not that we find the final answer; it's that we keep thinking about these things."[2] That's actually a pretty savvy business plan. Phillips is no dummy. He, like every other great philosopher-turned-entrepreneur, knows the secret to good philosophical discussion is to keep the questions coming. The danger of arriving at answers is that one might just put the philosophy business out of business. So finding isn't the point; seeking is.

Does that not, however, create a bit of a quandary? What good is a pursuit of truth if discovery is not the goal? Furthermore, what good is a pursuit of truth if discovery is not even possible? Why pursue that which cannot be attained? Why expend the intellectual energy in a search that has no possibility of ever ending? Is that not the ultimate exercise in futility? Are we supposed to chase, *Pepé Le Pew* style, after the elusive passion of our souls with no hope of ever catching her?

Any good philosopher worth his or her salt would answer that question with a resounding *Yes!* For while ultimate truth may never be fully attained, there is still much to be learned by the pursuit of it. That is the point of the Socrates Café: learning through the exchange of ideas. No one is ultimately right or wrong. Rather, all the participants are sharpened by the mutual sharing of each other's understanding of what truth is or is not.

But does that not beg even more questions? What is the nature of truth? Isn't truth elusive and mysterious? Isn't it impossible to attain? Or is truth knowable? Is there such a thing as ultimate truth? Is there a point where the searching ends and the simple adjusting to truth's immoveable realities begins? Those are indeed the questions of the ages.

GREAT MINDS THINK ALIKE

Reflecting on truth has historically been left to the great minds of philosophers and poets. Consider some of the musings on truth from these legendary thinkers and communicators:

* *Philosophy is the science which considers truth.* (Aristotle)
* *Truth is always about something, but reality is that about which truth is.* (C. S. Lewis)
* *It takes two to speak truth—one to speak, and another to hear.* (Henry David Thoreau)
* *There's a world of difference between truth and facts. Facts can obscure the truth.* (Maya Angelou)
* *Have patience a while; slanders are not long-lived. Truth is the child of time; ere long she shall appear to vindicate thee.* (Immanuel Kant)
* *No pleasure is comparable to the standing upon the vantage ground of truth.* (Francis Bacon)
* *Men occasionally stumble on the truth, but most of them pick themselves up and hurry off as if nothing had happened.* (Winston Churchill)

❀ *Telling the truth...is not solely a matter of moral character; it is also a matter of correct appreciation of real situations and of serious reflection upon them.* (Dietrich Bonhoeffer)

❀ *God offers to every mind its choice between truth and repose. Take which you please; you can never have both.* (Ralph Waldo Emerson)

❀ *God is truth and light his shadow.* (Plato)

❀ *The great enemy of the truth is very often not the lie—deliberate, contrived, and dishonest—but the myth—persistent, persuasive, and unrealistic.* (John F. Kennedy)

❀ *It is one thing to show a man that he is in error, and another to put him in possession of truth.* (John Locke)

❀ *There are no eternal facts, as there are no absolute truths.* (Friedrich Nietzsche)

❀ *The search for truth is more precious than its possession.* (Albert Einstein)

I find those comments fascinating. Did you notice what they all have in common? The reflections on truth by some of the world's greatest minds were only *about* truth. They talked about what truth does, how it acts, the impact it has, the way it should be treated, the rewards it brings and its priceless value. But none ventured into the murky depths of *defining* truth. None of them seemed willing to lay their cards on the table and say what truth *is*. Nietzsche came close, but he only managed to say what truth *is not*. Why is that? Is the meaning of truth so obscure? Or is truth just relative—like beauty—and found ultimately in the eye of its beholder? And, as stated by Einstein, is discovering truth not really the point? Are we human beings better off with the core belief that truth is always just beyond our reach, and therefore, we must continue to always reach beyond ourselves? Are we to be satisfied only with truth's search? Are we indeed asking too much if we also want truth's ultimate meaning?

HE HELD TRUTH TO BE SELF-EVIDENT

I would like to add another name to the list of those who have reflected and commented on truth. But I offer the name from a distinct standpoint: this thinker didn't stop at saying what truth was like. He boldly declared what truth was. This figure in history, untrained and relatively uneducated, didn't keep the definition of ultimate reality at a safe, conversational distance. He repeatedly offered up line after line of truth anecdotes. He never said what he *thought* truth was; he only said what he *knew* it to be. Truth, for this man, was not something you pursue; it pursued you. It was not something you create; it created you. And truth, according to this person, was clearly knowable, tangible and, by necessity, attainable.

Who was this outspoken philosopher? Jesus Christ, the carpenter from Nazareth, who lived over two millennia ago. And what was this truth that he talked about so boldly? It was the reality of God, his Father, as revealed in and modeled by Jesus himself.

Jesus Christ said things about truth that no one else dared to. He was no mere student or seeker of truth; he said he *was* truth. Now you and I both know that a person who walks around today claiming to be truth is very likely to get a one-way ticket to a gated community for the mentally retired. But let's not write off Jesus so quickly. Has he not, at least through his historical longevity alone, earned a hearing? Should we not grant him an audience just based on the uniqueness of his claims?

I'm inviting you to do so. In this book, I want to offer you a survey of Jesus' view of truth. I offer it to you for your assistance. I want to provide a tool for you to use while contemplating, not just the audacious teachings and claims of Jesus, but also the ultimate meaning of truth. And I'll use as my reference the greatest philosophical analysis of Jesus that has ever been written.

A THINKER'S THINKER

Believe it or not, some of the most profound philosophical and theosophical writing in the New Testament of the Bible came from a fisherman-turned-disciple named John. John and his brother James had been early disciples of John the Baptist before accepting the call to become followers of Jesus. John was an eyewitness to Jesus' ministry, death and purported resurrection. He wrote his account of Jesus' life after about sixty years of reflecting on what he saw and heard in Jesus.

John's work is clearly the most theologically oriented of the four accounts of Jesus' life in the Bible. It was a book written to both Jews and Greeks, but with special emphasis given to the thinkers and truth seekers in those crowds. John's account of Jesus' life is less chronological and more topical. He argued that Jesus was indeed God's Son and he used Jesus' teachings and miracles (John calls them *signs*) to support his thesis. It is a fascinating read.

Consider John's opening statement: "In the beginning was the Word, and the Word was with God, and the Word was God" (John 1:1).[3] This packed sentence immediately piqued the interest of both Greek and Hebrew thinkers in John's audience. Greeks believed in a concept known as *logos*—a thought or idea that transcended all other thoughts and ideas. They believed that one might discover or uncover logos by deep and profound reflection. As logos gradually became known, the wisdom, learning and overall condition of men would increase.

Hebrews also believed in logos, but theirs was no abstract entity. Logos was God's ultimate word or message. When spoken or revealed, it was to be immediately obeyed. God had offered initial logos in the Ten Commandments, but the prophets throughout the centuries had encouraged the Hebrews to look for a final, supreme logos, to be revealed later in the form of the Christ, or the Promised One. That logos would be the complete and final revelation of God to man.

In John's beautifully crafted statement, he wove together both the Greek and Hebrew concepts of logos (Our English term "Word," used in John 1:1, is the Greek word *logos*, so the verse more literally reads: "In the beginning was the logos, and the logos was with God, and the logos was God.") John argued that logos was eternal, that logos, like God, actually existed before creation and was the source of creation, that logos was in fellowship with God and that logos was somehow equal to God. With those lofty assertions, John immediately had the attention of two completely different audiences. Not bad work for one little sentence. Now here's the zinger: John claimed that Jesus was the logos, and he did so because he heard Jesus claim the same on more occasions than he could count.

Why Should You Keep Reading?

If you keep reading, I believe you'll be intrigued and challenged by the language and thoughts of Jesus as recorded by John. For instance, in John 8:40, Jesus identified himself as "a man who has told you the truth that I heard from God." That's a great example of Jesus' no-holds-barred approach to truth teaching. He claimed not only to know what truth was, but also to have acquired such knowledge from God himself.

In the following pages, we will examine Jesus' rather in-your-face statements on truth. We will look at what Jesus claimed was the truth about God, religion, Heaven, love, the nature of evil, truth itself and his own nature. In doing so, we will see that Jesus had some rather lofty ideas about these subjects, and he had even loftier thoughts about his connection to each. Every chapter concludes with questions you can use either personally or in a group setting to further explore Jesus' teachings on the given subject.

When you finish the book, you'll at least have a better understanding of the person of Christ. His messages are so controversial and scandalous that they tend to get watered down for the sake of ecumenical palatability and theological correctness. But Jesus was not concerned with being agreeable or safe. He clearly had a mindset of *letting the chips fall* when it came to his take on truth. And he did indeed let the chips fall, because his teachings on truth ended up getting him executed.

So if you keep reading, you will no doubt have better insight into who Jesus was and why he remains such an inflammatory figure in history. I believe, however, that if you keep reading, you may well discover more—much more.

POINTS FOR PONDERING

Do you consider yourself a religious person? Why or why not?

Do you have a history of exposure to or involvement in the church or some other type of religious activity?

Would you describe yourself as a spiritual seeker? In other words, are you open to and even curious about the possibility that spiritual realities exist beyond what you currently know or understand?

Why are you reading this book?

What is your opinion today of Jesus Christ?

CHAPTER 2

Something Sure Happened (The Truth about Truth)

• • •

It stands 307 feet tall, some six feet of bragging rights taller than its nearby neighbor, the Texas state capital. Each side is fifty-nine feet wide and has its own twelve-foot-diameter clock dotting its top. There is also a fifty-six-bell carillon, the highest in the state, with the largest bell weighing over seven thousand pounds. I am talking about the tower in the center of the University of Texas (UT) campus in Austin. Completed in 1937, the tower is a major Austin landmark and it represents the pride and excellence of the school it watches over.

Etched in stone across the entrance to the tower and viewed by hundreds of thousands of students, faculty and visitors each year is the phrase, "Ye shall know the truth and the truth shall make you free." Academicians still argue over whether education alone can lead to ultimate truth, or whether such fields as science, philosophy and even religion must come into play. I suspect that the debate is not likely to be settled anytime soon. Most do agree, however, that the bold inscription on the UT tower does state well the ultimate goal of education: the pursuit of truth. Academics, when stripped of political and social agendas, are at least partially about the struggle to discover truth. A noble pursuit indeed. The stone-etched statement is a good summation of the goal—and the desired result—of learning.

So here's an interesting question: Who said it? Who is quoted on the UT tower? What scholar, philosopher, scientist or politician first made those words famous, and what did he or she mean? What was truth, according to his or her point of view, and how was it discovered? And what was freedom? Did the speaker mean freedom from political or religious tyranny, or freedom that comes with having an educated mind? Was the author referring to emotional, intellectual or spiritual enlightenment? Knowing who the speaker was might help us gain some insight into what he or she considered truth and freedom to be. So look at the following list and see whom you might pick as our now-immortalized thinker:

* Mahatma Gandhi
* Albert Einstein
* The Prophet Mohammad
* Margaret Thatcher
* Abraham Lincoln
* Isaac Newton
* Blaise Pascal
* None of the above

Actually, the real answer may surprise you. It was Jesus. He who spoke such sentiments about truth was none other than the humble carpenter-turned-prophet who lived in Palestine over two thousand years ago. He was the religious teacher who claimed that truth could be known and that it set us free.

Isn't it a bit ironic that the opponents of Christianity ridicule it as a religion for dummies and the intellectually challenged?

Atheist leaders call for a rejection of the Christian faith because it is antithetical to reason and higher thought. And yet, here we have one of the greatest academic institutions in the world quoting the founder of the world's largest religion on the architectural center-piece of its campus.

I wonder how that one slipped by the building committee.

Does knowing Jesus is the source change how you view this statement? Does it seem strange to you that a world-renowned institution of higher learning would have the words of a religious leader boldly emblazoned on a major campus landmark? Does it matter that those whom Jesus was trying to reach rejected and publicly executed him as a common criminal? And does it matter that Jesus founded what is not only the largest but also arguably the most exclusive religion in the world? Does that seem consistent with the goals of higher education?

Well, herein lies the quandary of the ages: What is truth? How is it defined? Can it be known? And what did Jesus possibly think he knew about ultimate realities? What does a man who lived over two millennia ago have in common with the goals of today's highly sophisticated academic community? Did Jesus really have special insight into truth, or was he just another well-meaning but mistaken religious leader whose significance should and will fade with time? And perhaps most important of all: What is truth, and can it be known?

IF THE TRUTH BE KNOWN

Whether you believe him or not, you have to acknowledge that Jesus came out swinging when it came to discussions of truth. He was not shy about claiming to have the inside track on ultimate realities. He did not hesitate to call others wrong and insist that he was right when it came to such lofty matters. He even went so far as to say that he had a monopoly on understanding truth and that it could not be attained without his assistance.

Those are audacious, if not arrogant, claims. Perhaps that is why so many today write off Jesus as a kind, but loony, religious leader. Nobody with any sense walks around claiming to have the inside track on all matters of life, especially someone who ended up dying like Jesus did.

So what's behind it? What drove this first-century prophet to make such sweeping statements about reality...statements that he said applied to all centuries? And why should you care? Countless crazy people in history have made even crazier claims about their connections to the cosmos. Why should Jesus' warrant our attention?

I COULDN'T HAVE SAID IT BETTER MYSELF

I met Loyd Hampton while our church was purchasing his house and thirty-five-acre tract on the western edge of Austin. The city was closing in around him far too much for his liking. Several hundred acres of fresh land and the lure of less city noise were calling Loyd out to Lampasas, a small town about an hour north-west of Austin. Loyd had a PhD and worked for the University of Texas Jake Pickle Research Center for nearly forty years. He was the director of the applied research laboratory at the Pickle center when he retired. In short, Loyd was a brilliant scientist. Loyd's wife, Nan, had also earned a PhD and she taught genetics at UT. This was one smart couple. I am certain that their combined intelligence quotient would soar well above a perfect bowling score.

Loyd was a nature lover, and he wanted to make sure that our church had noble intentions for his thirty-five acres. He did not want to see it turned into a parking lot. As a result, we spent significant time together walking his land and talking about not just our church's plans, but also our church's beliefs and mission. Over time, Loyd and I became friends.

A year or so after Loyd moved to Lampasas, he invited me out to see his new spread. This meant a full day with Loyd and his two Great Danes, walking and romping through acre after acre of pristine Texas hill country. It also meant hours of uninterrupted conversation; and that, to me, was hard to pass up.

You see, Loyd was an agnostic. I liked Loyd and I was very curious about his lack of affinity for my belief system. It seemed like such a strange paradox to me: he wanted the church to have his land; he liked, trusted and respected me; he read our church business plan cover to cover and even sent copies of it to his children; but he didn't even come close to buying into our faith. The brief "religious" talks we had in the past were exciting and stimulating. I could only wonder what several hours in the open country might bring.

I gladly accepted Loyd's invitation and warned him that I clearly had an agenda. I would walk, but he had to agree to talk about spiritual matters. We had a delightful day together and I really enjoyed our time on his property. Loyd may not have believed in God, but he had no problem appreciating the beauty of creation. A few hours after lunch, we sat down with the Great Danes on Loyd's front porch. He offered me a cold Shiner Bock to go with the one he was having. (Shiner is a little German town southwest of Austin that houses a world-famous brewery.) Now I'm not in the habit of drinking beer while on duty, especially when I intend to lead my day-trip companion into a deep and profound discussion of spiritual truth. However, it did seem to mean a lot to Loyd, and it was really hot, and I didn't want to offend him, and I was really thirsty...so I accepted the Shiner—actually, two of them.

Anyway, after about thirty minutes of dancing around our subject, I finally just blurted out what I was thinking:

"Loyd, bottom-line it for me. What's your take on Jesus Christ?"

I know that's rather blunt; I think the Shiner may have emboldened me a bit.

"Well," he said, "I don't believe we can ever know for certain what happened."

Then after a few short moments of silence, Loyd politely belched and added, "But something sure as hell happened."

I couldn't have said it better myself.

I think the reason that most religious skeptics are willing to give Jesus a hearing is because it is hard to deny that something really did happen. The significant historical and archeological evidence, two thousand years of church history and changed lives, and the survival, expansion and eventual success of the early church over its powerful Roman adversary is more than enough to give even the most cynical skeptic pause. Something happened indeed. Genuine seekers of truth compromise the integrity of their search by not giving Jesus his day in court. And when considered in their original context, his statements about truth raise some intriguing spiritual questions. And, I will argue, they offer even more intriguing answers.

WHAT IS TRUTH?

It was a cool morning outside the courthouse. The sun was beginning to make its daily appearance just off the eastern edge of the mountains, but it had not yet risen high enough to remove the chill from the air. *Honestly,* the governor thought, *I doubt even the sun's full heat could take the chill off this day.*

Standing directly before the governor was the bound prisoner. The two stood very close, making quiet, almost whispered conversation. They were a strange study in contrasts: The governor, no doubt holding all the cards, seemed nervous and unsettled. The prisoner, knowing that the governor could not possibly rule in his favor and spare his life, seemed oddly at ease.

If their appearance was strange, their conversation was even more so. It bordered on the philosophical; they were discussing truth:

GOVERNOR: *Look, I need to know the truth about you. You were brought before me because you keep talking about your own kingdom. You have made too many of the wrong people mad and pushed too many of the wrong buttons. Tell me who you really are so I can help you.*

PRISONER: *My kingdom has nothing to do with this world. It's not really something you can understand right now. Perhaps later.*

GOVERNOR: *So you really think you are a king? Please tell me that you don't really believe that.*

PRISONER: *I am a king. It's why I came into the world. I came to set up my kingdom and to help people see the truth. In fact, you need to know this: whoever is on the side of truth will listen to me.*

GOVERNOR: *Give me a break. Don't talk to me about truth. You know how many prisoners have stood before me begging for their lives, and doing so in the name of truth? You can't possibly imagine how many versions of the so-called truth I hear in one day. And then you come along and have the audacity to tell me that you really do rule a kingdom and that it is based on truth. You...this rejected, pathetic prophet...dare to stand here and talk to me about truth? You really are nuts. Well, here is something that you need to know, Your Majesty: I learned the truth a long time ago. You know what it is? It is that truth, if it even exists, is slippery, evasive and very relative. All people have their own version of it; some even have two! For me, I have quit trying to figure it out. I have given up on truth.* (For the more literal version of this conversion between Pilate and Jesus, see John 18:33–38.)

Maybe you can relate to Pilate's cynicism. I certainly can. In a day and age where just about anything goes in spiritual discussions, where straight-faced adults pray to everything from trees to aliens to frogs, and in a world where everyone seems willing to opine about the frivolous and yet no one is willing to offer meaningful answers on the really hard questions—like why daddies abandon their daughters, why there is tribal genocide, why the rich won't share with the poor, why mudslides take out entire villages or why children are born with severe birth defects—it is certainly easy to become skeptical about serious conversations on truth.

And yet there stood Jesus, a stark figure in history, making bold and comprehensive remarks about what is ultimately real. That is why I think we owe him a hearing. Think about it: the man stood bound and bleeding before the judge who could condemn him, and yet he talked about his kingdom.

Now one of two things is probably true about a man like that. One, he's just plain crazy—well meaning, perhaps, but crazy. That is the case about 99.9 percent of the time. Or two, he's not crazy, and he knows something we don't know. That only happens about 0.1 percent of the time, or only once in history. Hmm…

Jesus' Take on Truth

John's gospel contains at least forty-seven verses that use the word *truth*. Dozens more use the word *true*. Jesus spoke all but a few of those references. The rest were spoken or written about him. In other words, every reference to truth in John is connected to Jesus.

John deliberately linked the discussion of truth with the discussion of Jesus. Those two discussions, for this follower-turned-biblical-writer, went hand in hand.

Jesus' comments on truth in John's gospel can easily be divided into three categories: (1) his "truly, truly" statements, (2) his comments on the nature of truth (3) and his controversial statements that link him with ultimate truth. If we are to come to a conclusion about Jesus, and either discard him as misguided or continue to pursue him as knowing something we do not, then some reflection on these statements is required.

Amen, Brother!

If you grew up with any church exposure or religious training, then you may be familiar with the 1611 King James translation of the Bible. Many of us cut our spiritual teeth reading *thee, thou, whither, ye,* and an assortment of other now out-of-date expressions found in the King James. It is a beautiful translation, but the words sound more like Shakespeare than a bunch of fishermen and tax collectors sitting around a fire.

Some of the most commonly known King James verses are the *Verily, verily* statements of Jesus found exclusively in John's gospel. The actual translated word is *amen*, and it simply means *true*.

When we say *amen* at the end of a prayer, we are asserting that everything we have just said in the prayer is true. We are claiming that our prayers are true, authentic and will pass God's sniff test. Our *amen* means that our hearts are sincere in seeking God.

When people say *amen* during a sermon or in response to a statement someone has made, they are attesting to the truth of what they just heard. They could have just as easily said *True*, or in today's parlance, *Word*.

Jesus had the unusual and unique habit of beginning his teachings with *Amen, amen,* or *Truly, truly*. He would lead with it, as if to tell his audience to listen up, because what followed was very important. When Jesus used his *truly, truly* formula, he wasn't just stating that what he was about to say was true, like one might swear to before a courtroom testimony; he was saying that it was Truth—an eternal principle, a timeless reality, something that could not be ignored.

Consider some of Jesus' *truly, truly* assertions:

- *Truly, truly, I say to you, you will see heaven opened, and the angels of God ascending and descending on the Son of Man* [a reference to himself]. (John 1:51)
- *Truly, truly, I say to you, unless one is born again, he cannot see the kingdom of God.* (John 3:3)
- *Truly, truly, I say to you, the Son can do nothing of his own accord, but only what he sees the Father doing. For whatever the Father does, that the Son does likewise.* (John 5:19)
- *Truly, truly, I say to you, whoever hears my word and believes him who sent me has eternal life. He does not come into judgment, but has passed from death to life.* (John 5:24)
- *Truly, truly, I say to you, unless you eat the flesh of the Son of Man and drink his blood, you have no life in you.* (John 6:53)
- *Truly, truly, I say to you, if anyone keeps my word, he will never see death.* (John 8:51)

- *Truly, truly, I say to you, whoever believes in me will also do the works that I do; and greater works than these will he do, because I am going to the Father.* (John 14:12)
- *Truly, truly, I say to you, whatever you ask of the Father in my name, he will give it to you.* (John 16:23)

Those are some fairly radical assertions. Jesus must have been one bold hombre to make such declarations. But hold on, it only gets worse.

TRUTH EXPLAINED

Jesus didn't just claim to reveal truth; he claimed to be an expert on it. Jesus spoke of truth like a professional craftsman might speak of his trade. He acted and sounded like he had insider information on the whole truth thing. Keep in mind that Jesus ministered in a day and culture when seeking truth was quite in vogue; finding it, however, was a different matter. But not for Jesus; he talked about truth like he had grown up with it. For example:

- *God is spirit, and those who worship him must worship in spirit and truth.* (John 4:24)
- *If you abide in my word, you are truly my disciples, and you will know the truth, and the truth will set you free.* (John 8:31–32)
- *But now you seek to kill me, a man who has told you the truth that I heard from God.* (John 8:40)
- *You are of your father the devil, and your will is to do your father's desires. He was a murderer from the beginning, and has nothing to do with the truth, because there is no truth in him. When he lies, he speaks out of his own character, for he is a liar*

and the father of lies. But because I tell the truth, you do not believe me. (John 8:44–45)

✦ *When the Spirit of truth comes, he will guide you into all the truth, for he will not speak on his own authority, but whatever he hears he will speak, and he will declare to you the things that are to come.* (John 16:13)

✦ *Sanctify them in the truth; your word is truth* [spoken in a prayer to God]. (John 17:17)

✦ *For this purpose I was born and for this purpose I have come into the world—to bear witness to the truth. Everyone who is of the truth listens to my voice.* (John 18:37)

Did you notice how unintimidated Jesus was by the subject of truth? He did not speak as someone who was still wondering where truth begins and ends. His take on truth seems so personal, so advanced. One has to wonder where Jesus got all his ideas on the matter. Even if you disagree with him, you have to at least acknowledge that it doesn't sound as if he was making these things up as he went. Jesus' comments on the nature of truth, albeit controversial, sound as if he was speaking from a deep reservoir of personal knowledge; or, at least he thought he was.

TRUTH PERSONIFIED

I mentioned earlier that Jesus' statements on truth could be lumped into three categories—his *truly, truly* statements, his teachings about truth and those statements where he connected truth with himself. It is this third grouping that clearly sets Jesus apart from other well-known religious leaders and teachers.

Most religious leaders point beyond themselves to something other or something greater. They include themselves as being on the journey to discover truth and offer instructions and insights on how to get there. Not Jesus. He brazenly pointed back to himself and basically said, "If you want to know truth, look no further. It is standing right before you." In short, Jesus linked truth to himself. His most notorious "I-equal-truth" statement is found in John 14:6, "Jesus answered, 'I am the way and the truth and the life. No one comes to the Father except through me.'"

Scholars and skeptics alike have gone to great extremes to unpack and disarm this over-the-top declaration of Jesus. By far, this statement has created the most controversy for Christianity. It seems too narrow and exclusive. No wonder people take issue with it. Jesus would be much more palatable and would fit better into the synchronistic religious landscape if he wasn't credited with such an outlandish statement. As a result, many throughout history have worked overtime to remove the stinging implications of Jesus' claim. I, for one, feel no need to come to Jesus' rescue here or try to diffuse this rather contentious comment. This man not only claimed to be God but also accepted worship as God. That being the case, this statement doesn't seem so out of place for him.

Please don't reduce Christ's comments to something that he did not intend them to be. Jesus wasn't stupid. He knew full well the implications of claiming to be "the way to God" in a highly monotheistic society. This was no slip of Jesus' tongue; it needs no spin-doctor to clean it up. Jesus meant what he said. To do justice to our investigation of him, we can't afford to dilute his comments.

Jesus wanted his audience to believe that he was truth revealed, truth with skin on it. He wanted men and women to point their respective searches for ultimate reality squarely in his direction, and then to stop when they got to him. He claimed that if seekers of purpose, meaning and truth bet the spiritual farm on him, they would indeed find what they were looking for.

That's pretty high cotton for a small-town carpenter.

A MAN WHO TOLD US THE TRUTH

While the world seems no closer to reaching an agreed-to definition of truth, the brief lifespan and even briefer ministry of Jesus offers some interesting fodder for the dialogue. Let's acknowledge that Jesus had some astounding things to say about a topic that has intrigued philosophers, poets, scientists and scholars for centuries.

Jesus believed that truth was not abstract, but clearly definable, discernible and knowable. He argued that the discovery of truth was inseparably linked not just to knowing God, but also to knowing himself. He declared that not only were his words true and accurate, but they also revealed eternal truth to us. And, he claimed to be a man who told us the truth that he heard from God.

Well, if you ever happen to be in Austin and you have time to stop by the UT campus, go to the tower and read the inscription. You now know who said it and you know to what truth he was referring. Jesus was not talking about the outcome of a good education; he was talking about himself. Only when men and women are in relationship with him are they truly free—that is what Jesus claimed.

POINTS FOR PONDERING

What is your current definition of truth?

Do you believe in ultimate realities? Are there things in the universe that are unchanging? If so, could those be considered truths?

Is morality objective? Or are there really moral absolutes in the world? If so, where do they come from?

How do you feel about rather audacious claims? Could there really be a man in history who knew more than everyone else? Could Jesus have been that man?

If Jesus was mistaken or deluded about truth and his relationship to it, what does that mean for the Christian religion as a whole?

What is your opinion today of Jesus Christ?

CHAPTER 3

The God I Want to Believe (The Truth about God)

• • •

I HAD BEEN HIKING FOR nearly an hour when I first saw him. As I popped up over a knoll on the approach to the lake, I walked right up on him. He was lying on his stomach in the snow, almost completely spread-eagle. He seemed as startled to see me as I was to see him. It was almost as if I had caught him in an embarrassing moment…actually I had.

It was early June and I was taking my first hike of the season, just west of Estes Park, Colorado. I was on the trail from Glacier Gorge to Sky Pond, a nine-mile trek that is spectacularly gorgeous and easy enough to be a good warm-up hike. June in the Rockies is still unofficially springtime, and there was snow everywhere. I had just reached the first lake of three on the trail when I discovered Michael Murray struggling in the snow. He had apparently fallen and then rolled onto his stomach in an effort to put his feet back under him.

Michael looked to be a very underprepared hiker. He carried no pack, had no food or water and he was hiking alone. (Actually, I was alone too, but I wasn't lying facedown in the snow!) Besides all that, Michael was seventy-three years old.

"Oh, hello there," he said, "I wonder if you can tell me how to get to Sky Pond." He was so calm and polite that you would have thought that it was perfectly normal for a septuagenarian to be out frolicking in the snow, in the woods, in the mountains, without a pack, miles away from civilization.

"Yes, I can," I replied. "Actually I am going there myself. How about I just walk with you for a while." I was convinced that finding Sky Pond was going to be the *least* of his problems. He seemed genuinely grateful for my assistance, and so off we went.

The trail around the first lake, a large beauty called Loch Vale, is relatively gentle. The easygoing trek gave me the chance to set a friendly pace and talk with my new companion. He lived in Boulder, had little family and was retired. He enjoyed hiking and had decided on this day to take on the deep snow that still graced the mountains. Considering how wet and tired he looked, the snow appeared to be winning.

We made small talk and I found Michael to be friendly and amiable. He also cussed like a sailor, which for some reason seemed out of character for a man his age. After about thirty minutes of safe dialogue, I decided to spice up our conversation a bit. I wanted to ask Michael about his faith—to see what, if anything, he believed. Boulder is much like my hometown of Austin: people tend to be quite spiritual, but they are often skeptical of any specific or organized belief system. I was curious whether Michael shared that skepticism.

After more than twenty years of discussing spiritual matters with complete strangers, I have learned not to just dive right in with, "What do you think of God, the universe and all related subjects?" It tends to overwhelm folks. So I tossed Michael some bait and waited to see if he would bite:

"Why do you enjoy hiking?"

It may seem like an innocent question, but very few people hike because they love blisters and sore muscles. There is usually some deeper and more profound allure. Michael was no exception:

"Water music and great vistas."

I knew exactly what Michael meant by "water music." Few things are more musical than the sounds of a gentle mountain stream or a raging mountain river. My dad used to say that the sound "sure cures what ails ya." It really is a salve for the soul.

Now here is where the bait part kicks in. I didn't respond to Michael's answer. I just kept walking, genuinely reflecting on his comment. But the growing silence between us seemed to beg him to reciprocate and ask about my reasons for hiking. He eventually did: "What about you? Why do you enjoy hiking?"

Bait firmly taken, I proceeded ever so gently:

"Well, I can certainly identify with water music and great vistas. But I also really sense God out here. Some of my most profound God-moments have been in the mountains. So for me, hiking is kind of a spiritual exercise."

What happened next was amazing. Michael suddenly developed boot trouble. He stopped and sat right down in the snow. As he was adjusting his snowshoes he said, "Hey, I'm slowing you down and I need to fix my boots. You go on ahead." It wasn't a request; it was a command. My seemingly gentle spiritual nudge had pushed the wrong button for Michael. It was obvious that he wanted no part of a conversation with spiritual overtones. He would apparently rather get lost in the mountains than be required to converse about God.

I offered Michael some final instructions to Sky Pond and then I pushed on. And as quickly as I had found Michael, I had lost him.

CONVERSATION-KILLING 101

It is amazing how quickly a God reference can shut down an otherwise meaningful conversation. My abrupt end with Michael is no isolated exception. People tend to shy away from genuine spiritual dialogue, especially with strangers. Now at first that might seem normal, with faith and religion being such personal matters. But when you stop and think about the topics we are willing to engage others in—sexual orientation and preferences, political persuasions, pro-life or pro-choice, foreign and domestic issues, and even Ford versus Chevy and rock 'n' roll versus country—one has to wonder why so many avoid showing their spiritual cards. More specifically, why are open discussions of God so hard to come by? Personal experience has certainly shown me that if I want to kill a party, ruin a business luncheon, or for that matter, rid myself of a hiking partner, all I have to do is mention the divine. That is usually when things start going south.

Why is that? Why is God such a conversational no-no? What makes honest interaction about God so taboo? And why has such dialogue been relegated to confessionals and Sunday-school classes? I would like to suggest some reasons.

People don't really know what they believe. They tend to be much better informed and more articulate about Wall Street and weather patterns. As a result, they are hesitant to make conversation about God and risk appearing ignorant about such an obviously important subject.

People know what they believe, but they don't live by it. Many have strong convictions and beliefs about God, but they have shelved them for convenience's sake. Were they to vocalize their actual belief system, their words would be self-indicting, since their actions don't follow suit.

People have serious God baggage. Some can't say *God* without getting a bad taste in their mouths. What was portrayed before them, done to them or spoken at them in God's name was more than enough to cause them to bury any remaining God-desires. Bringing God back up simply isn't worth the pain that it would cause.

People are mad at God. Billionaire media mogul Ted Turner was raised in a Catholic-Episcopal home and actually planned to be a missionary. When he was twenty, his teenage sister died from a rare form of lupus. Turner, who had prayed thirty minutes a day for her healing, wrote off God. Said Turner, "A kind and loving God wouldn't let my sister suffer so much. I said, 'I don't want to have anything to do with you.'" Today, Turner claims to be agnostic.[4] Can you relate? Most of the agnostics and atheists I have been privileged to know are really just so mad at or wounded by God that they will not allow themselves to even acknowledge his existence.

DESIGNER GODS

Trying to understand God is a noble venture in today's mix-and-match culture. The current trend is away from a singular view of the divine. Narrowing God down to one reality is a bit hard to swallow for many of today's spiritual seekers. Unlike many of our European neighbors who practice a strict cultural monotheism, Westerners feel no such loyalty to one view of God. Jeremiah Creedon wrote, "Though nine out of ten American adults believe that God exists, there's growing disagreement about how God should be described. God is Michelangelo's bearded old man in the Sistine Chapel. God is pure intelligence. God is cosmic energy. God is Goddess."[5]

Pulitzer Prize winning writer and former Los Angeles Dodgers owner Frank McCourt agreed. In a *Life* magazine article, McCourt argued that the consumer mind-set of the West has finally taken over religion. Customers feel no need to limit themselves to one brand or flavor of God. When everything else in life competes for their attention and has to make the best offer to get their business, why shouldn't theology be the same?

McCourt sees great benefit in the buffet-like culture that has developed in Western religion. He wrote: "Americans, answerable only to their God, can choose. The sweet irony is that America has become a most God-fearing nation. By allowing the garden to grow as it will, we enjoy a multifarious bounty—one nation under *Gods*."[6] (Emphasis mine.)

I certainly can see the attraction of such reasoning. Who wouldn't enjoy a relationship with a made-to-order deity? Many today prefer the synchronistic approach to faith that allows them to dabble in elements of the various religions that most appeal to them. This "thirty-one-flavors" methodology chooses the best, most attractive aspects of a religious system and sets the less attractive aside. The result is a custom-built ideology that is quick to comfort and quick to approve, but rarely challenges. The payoff of the spiritual smorgasbord is that it almost always takes on the image of its creator; the irony being that the "creator" is usually the seeker.

While I understand the allure of such theology, I question its wisdom. What good is the pursuit of truth if we predetermine the outcome before we even begin the search? Why bother seeking God if we are only seeking the parts of God that fit our lifestyle? Where is the courage or the integrity in a spiritual pursuit that only wants to discover that which is convenient or palatable?

If it is God whom we indeed seek, then we cannot set predetermined limits around what we are willing to find. Authentic scientific pursuits do not limit allowable outcomes to what is consistent with what is already known or believed. If that were the case, we would still believe in a flat earth that is at the center of its own universe. I am afraid, however, that many Westerners aren't willing to make the leap to a spiritual universe of which they are not at the center. Most of us still prefer God to orbit around us, not us around him. As a result, we define God even before we discover him. Authentic theology must allow God to reveal himself as he really is, not as we want him to be.

SETTING THE RECORD STRAIGHT

Jesus taught extensively about God. Given the culture in which he lived, that was no small matter. While monotheism dominated Jewish leaders' thinking, their Roman and Greek counterparts embraced rampant polytheism. There was no lack of "professional" instruction on the subject of God or gods. So what could Jesus possibly have to offer on such a lofty topic as the divine? What did a locally educated carpenter have to say about God? And what gave him the right to say it? There were certainly plenty of "Who does this guy think he is?" responses to Jesus' messages, yet he found sympathetic audiences with people from all types of cultural, religious and social backgrounds. Something about Jesus' teachings on God clicked with his hearers. That "click" may have been Jesus' attempts to paint a fresh picture of God—a picture, by the way, that Jesus claimed to have seen firsthand.

The Jews of Jesus' day were still stinging from seventy years of national exile in Babylon, even though it had occurred four hundred years earlier. For a nation whose identity and theology were wrapped up in geography, exile was a fate worse than death. After the exile, they returned to Jerusalem determined to never again fall into the idolatry and empty religious practices that had cost them so dearly before. Their unforgiving adherence to man-made rules created an image of God that was not the least bit inviting. The shoot-first-and-don't-bother-to-ask-questions-later God they promoted did succeed in striking fear in the hearts of their followers, but that's about all. Real devotion was lost in the translation.

The gods of Greek and Roman mythology were nothing more than glorified humans, and badly behaved ones at that. These "gods" lied, cheated, murdered and were highly self-absorbed. They showed little interest in the plight of humans and offered little hope for them.

Thus, when Jesus showed up proclaiming the kingdom of God, he played initially to skeptical ears. The skepticism didn't last long. Jesus' portrayal of God was starkly different from what religious seekers had been taught for centuries. Jesus actually made God seem...*appealing*. It was like Jesus was on a personal mission to set the record straight about God.

A Good God

Jesus drilled down on what he thought was the heart and character of God. The God he described was so countercultural that his message soon became wildly popular with the common people. We need to consider those attributes of God that Jesus highlighted. But before we do, let me offer an overview of some of Jesus' broader assertions about God:

* *God rules in a kingdom.* (John 3:3, 5)
* *God is spirit and must be worshiped in spirit and truth.* (John 4:24)

+ *God is unique. There are no other gods besides him.* (John 5:44)
+ *God speaks to people, and his voice can be heard.* (John 8:47)
+ *God deserves glory and is glorified by the work he does in the earth.* (John 9:3; 11:40)
+ *God has a will that can be known and discerned. We choose to either obey or disobey his will.* (John 6:29; 7:17; 12:26)

None of these seem particularly surprising. You have probably heard these assertions about God before. Jesus' audience certainly had. But Jesus went well beyond the conventional wisdom about God. What he taught about God, if true, proved that God was radically different from how they had previously perceived him. The God that Jesus presented was attractive, heroic and innately good.

GOD AND LOVE

The most basic characteristic of the God of Jesus was love. Far from being the lightning-bolt-throwing, sinner-zapping demagogue that so many associated with God, the God that Jesus proclaimed was motivated and defined by his love—a love, by the way, that far exceeds any that we know or manifest as humans.

Jesus talked extensively about God's love. He said that God loved all people and wanted to save them from their wrong and self-destructive behaviors. When Jesus wanted to identify the most basic characteristic of God-honoring people, he said it was love. God's people should love each other, said Jesus, because God loves them.

In perhaps the most quoted verse in the Bible, Jesus said, "God so loved the world, that he gave his one and only Son" (John 3:16). The love that Jesus described in that statement is totally unique to his view of God. This love is unconditional, unwavering and unmerited. In a world where everything exists on a merit system (including, unfortunately, love and favor), such love is refreshing, to say the least. Jesus taught that God's love for humans was not based on their behavior, their morals or even their acceptance of him. He loved them, rather, because he had created them and placed his image within them. Even in the face of blanket skepticism and rejection, God still loves all humans. For Jesus, God was the perfect role model of love—he loves for the right reasons and without regard to the reciprocity of the objects of his love.

GOD AS GIVER

Jesus also taught that God was the ultimate giver: "For God so loved the world, that he gave his only Son..." (John 3:16). I mentioned before that this may be the most frequently quoted and most recognizable verse in the Bible. As such, it has a curiously simple message. Reduce this verse to its basic subject and predicate, and it reads, "He gave." I find that a rather intriguing concept for such a profoundly theological religion as Christianity. At its core, Christianity (the faith that Jesus started) is about a giving God.

When you survey the gods of history, the gods of mythology and the gods of legend and lore, you find gods who were selfish and quick tempered, murderous and often evil. Because they were gods, they could do whatever they wanted, and they did. Their payoff for being gods was that they were entitled to make demands.

Thus, Jesus' picture of God is astounding. According to Jesus, God was entitled, God could make demands, God could do anything he wanted, and yet he didn't. Instead, the God of Jesus is the Great Giver.

Every major world religion has self at its center. They teach about improving, serving, changing and promoting the individual. The faith that Jesus created knows no such self-orientation. It's all about others, and the others-centeredness of Christianity originated in the heart of the God who refused to exercise his divine privilege, but rather emptied himself of all benefit so that he could live and die for others, even those who would reject him.

To say that Jesus' message about God was countercultural, counter theological and counter to everything that had been previously taught about God would be an understatement.

THE GOD WHO TOOK THE HIT

Not long ago, my employer changed insurance carriers. I was required to undergo a litany of tests to make sure that I was "insurable." On the appointed day, a female twentysomething showed up at my office, with portable lab in hand, ready to assault any number of my veins in the name of medical due diligence.

My young guest didn't really look the part of a nurse practitioner; at least she didn't look how I expected her to. With her bright-red hair, multiple nose and ear piercings and thick layers of black clothing, this girl looked like someone who indeed might have had much experience with needles. But my first impression of her proved to be wrong. She was smart, witty and very articulate.

It is funny how allowing someone to poke you with needles can make you feel immediately close to them. Maybe it's just a matter of the physical proximity involved. Personal space and boundaries fly right out the window when someone is checking your temperature, your pulse and your blood pressure and filling three vials with your blood. After a while, you somehow feel connected to them.

I decided to take advantage of this intimacy with my new friend and find out where she stood spiritually. After all, I *was* a pastor and she *was* in my office taking *my* blood. The least she could do was indulge my spiritual curiosity. After a few rounds of surface theological banter, I asked her about her view of God. Her answer astounded me. It went something like this:

I heard a story once about a man who worked for a train company. He staffed a junction booth at an old bridge that crossed over a river. He had to manually operate the rail switches on the dated bridge tracks or otherwise the train was likely to derail and go careening off the bridge.

The man had a preschool-age son who loved to accompany his daddy to work. He was fascinated by trains and enjoyed watching them as they passed by. Sometimes he'd even get to sit in his dad's lap and help operate the switch controls. It was the perfect playground for a little boy.

One day the boy was standing down by the river when a train was approaching the bridge. As the boy took a few steps out so he could better see the train, he tripped and tumbled headlong into the swirling waters. His father, seated in the control booth, saw the accident and knew immediately that he only had a few seconds to act before his son would be out of reach. He also knew with gut-wrenching clarity that he could not retrieve his son and get back to the booth in time to secure the train's safe passage over the bridge. If he went for his son, the train would probably derail, fly off the bridge and kill all the passengers on board. The engineers, crew and his company's customers were fully expecting him to be at his post when they passed by. Their lives were depending on it. If he stayed in the booth and manned the rail controls, his son would drown. In one heartrending moment, he knew what he had to do. The man turned his back to the river, gripped the rail controls and waited the excruciatingly long two minutes for the train to pass. When it had, the man sprinted from his booth and raced down to the water's edge. His son was gone.

After a brief pause, the girl continued:

I've been told that's what God did for me; basically he allowed his Son to die so I wouldn't have to. I'm not sure I understand it all, but if that's true, if that's what God is like, then that's the God I want to believe.

That, according to Jesus, is exactly what God is like. The God that Jesus described passionately and zealously loves us. He created us, placed his image within each of us and longs for an eternal relationship with us. He knew that we were trapped in our sin and that we would die therein if he did not act. He wasn't required to act. He didn't have to rescue us. But he was so motivated by his love that he could not sit idly by while we perished. He chose to take matters into his own holy hands. His answer was to pass judgment on his Son and offer mercy to us. There is no logic in that, for his Son was innocent and we were guilty, but that is what he did. He basically stayed at his post, securing our safe passage into his presence, all the while knowing that he was killing his Son in the process. That is the heart of the God Jesus proclaimed. Listen to it in his own words: "For God so loved the world that he gave his only Son, so that everyone who believes in him will not perish but have eternal life. God did not send his Son into the world to condemn it, but to save it" (John 3:16–17, New Living Translation).

A Man Who Told Us the Truth

Jesus had much more to say about God, and we will look at that in the next chapter. But to conclude this one, I would like to ask a question: If you were lost in the woods and a friendly hiker came by and offered to help you find your way home, but he wanted to discuss spiritual matters along the way, would you go with him or send him packing? I hope this chapter has helped you get your arms around some of the basic concepts of the God of Jesus—that he is loving, that he is a giver and that he took the hit for our sins—and that you might be more open to healthy spiritual dialogue about him.

Points for Pondering

Imagine that a seven-year-old asked you to describe God. What would you say?

Use as many adjectives as you can think of to describe the God you grew up with. Create a word picture of the God that was modeled for you or taught to you by your spiritual leaders.

How different is your view of God from that which Jesus described?

What do you think about Jesus' claim that God is loving, giving and sacrificial?

If you were confident that God was indeed a loving God, would you want to know more about him?

If you could be sure that God would hear you, what would you say to God right now?

What is your opinion today of Jesus Christ?

CHAPTER 4

The Dad of Your Dreams
(The Truth about Your Father)

• • •

SHE SPOKE THROUGH HER TEARS: "Can you use a different image for God? This whole father thing isn't really working for me." That was not the response I had expected.

In the early 1990s, I worked at a church in Fort Worth, Texas, in the shadow of the largest theological training institution in the world. I was completing my doctoral work and I enjoyed the exposure to other seminary students. My church eagerly opened its doors to these students, becoming their safe place before they went off to all parts of the globe in the name of Christian ministry.

I taught a Sunday school class for seminary students and their spouses. Each Sunday I would spend an hour interacting with fifty to sixty bright, talented and very committed young men and women. It was a privilege to be able to invest in these aspiring Christian leaders. It was also eye-opening, for as sold out to their cause as these students were, they were still a spiritually banged-up group. They loved God and were committed to serving him, but their view of God was not always healthy. And oddly enough, in most cases the culprit for their shortsighted thinking about God could be named in one word—dad.

On this particular Sunday morning, I was teaching on one of the Old Testament verses that likened God to a father. The eighth-century BC prophet Isaiah, in a text quoted frequently at Christmas and made famous in Handel's *Messiah*, called God the "Everlasting Father" (Isa. 9:6). I have always loved that image and I was talking about how God is the perfect dad: He will never grow old or die. He will never abandon or desert us. He will always be our Heavenly Father.

As I was talking, one of the women on the front row of the class began to weep openly. When I asked her what was wrong, she made the comment I referenced above. She could not see God as a good father. Actually, she didn't want to see God as any kind of father. Her experience with *father* was really bad. She could hardly speak the word without disdain spewing from her lips. The whole class could feel the hate and anger in this wounded person. "Dad" was a bad thing. She had no desire to think of God in such deplorable terms. *Can you pick a different image for God? This one isn't really working for me.*

DAD OR DUD?

Yes, I can pick a different image, but that wouldn't really solve this woman's problem. Because, like it or not, as little children we draw our first conclusions about God by what we see in our dad. That can be a frightening concept for a parent. When my children were younger, they looked at me and then naturally projected what they saw in me onto God. It wasn't a very good first picture, as I am far from perfect, but it was the one they had. Children tend to expect God to act like dad, and they will tend to have a limited view of God until they rethink him in light of who he really is. Beyond that, a child's relationship with God will often parallel their relationship with their dad. So for good or bad, right or wrong, the first impression we get of God is from our father.

Now think about this: In over thirty years of dialoguing with spiritual seekers, I have rarely met agnostics or atheists who claimed to have a healthy relationship with their fathers. It's uncanny to think about, but it's true. Whenever I meet people who are hostile toward God, I ask them about their relationships with their dads. Sometimes I get a noncommittal, "Oh, it was fine." But usually after some pressing, they reveal that things were not so peachy in the father department at home. Dad was abusive or dad was an alcoholic. Dad was a hypocritical religious fanatic. Dad was a philanderer. Sometimes they will tell me that their dads were agnostic or atheist. I then ask about *their dads'* dads (their grandfathers.) The pattern will be the same: they were abusive, killed in the war or ran off with other women. Subsequently, somewhere along the line, the spiritual seeker started expecting God to be just like dad; after all, doesn't God call himself the Heavenly *Father?* And like the young woman in the Sunday-school class, they determine that if God is indeed like a father, then based on their experience, they will just pass on the whole God thing. They have seen the father routine, and frankly, it wasn't all that great.

POSTTRAUMATIC DAD DISORDER

"I never knew my so-called father. He was a nonfactor—unless you count his absence as a factor. Just because he provided the DNA that made me doesn't make him my father, and as far as I'm concerned, there is no connection between us, absolutely no connection...I've never had a single conversation with my mother about him. Not once."

So wrote former seven-time Tour de France champion Lance Armstrong in his first book, *It's Not about the Bike*.[7] I am sure you know by now, Lance eventually admitted to doping throughout his career as a Tour competitor and was stripped of his seven titles. He now has the unfortunate reputation of being the greatest sports fraud in US history.

Now I have to tell you that I was a huge Lance Armstrong fan. I have done just enough cycling to know how remarkable his accomplishments were, drugs notwithstanding. In the early days of his career, I used to occasionally see him riding around Austin, either with teammates or just with an escort car. I would always honk and cheer. Lance was clearly one of my sports heroes.

To me, his story is one of great tragedy. Think of what he could have been.

Now I may be wrong, but I think Lance makes a great case for my whole *dad baggage equals God baggage* argument. According to Lance, not only was his real father a no-show, but his stepfather was a physically abusive parent and an adulterous husband. He was also an outspoken "Christian." Damage done, Lance concluded early on that religion was not all it was cracked up to be. He wrote, "I thought he [his stepfather] was an angry testosterone geek, and as a result, my early impression of organized religion was that it was for hypocrites."[8]

Based on what little I have read and heard about Lance's "dad" experiences, it sounds like he would have great difficulty trusting God. If our fathers really are our first impression of the Heavenly Father, then Lance is clearly zero for two in the God department. Who could blame him for not warming up to the invisible version of two really bad earthly models?

Lance makes no secret of his lack of interest in Christian matters. Even during his near-fatal bout with cancer, he found faith in God hard to come by. Consider the following:

> *I asked myself what I believed. I had never prayed a lot. I hoped hard, I wished hard, but I didn't pray. I had developed a certain distrust of organized religion growing up, but I felt I had the capacity to be a spiritual person, and to hold some fervent beliefs. Quite simply, I believed I had a responsibility to be a good person, and that meant fair, honest, hardworking and honorable. If I did that, if I was good to my family, true to my friends, if I gave back to the community or to some cause, if I wasn't a liar, a thief, or a cheat, then I believed that should be enough. At the end of the day, if there was indeed some Body or presence standing there to judge me, I hoped I would be judged on whether I had lived a true life, not on whether I believed in a certain book, or whether I'd been baptized. If there was indeed a God at the end of my days, I hoped he didn't say, "but you were never a Christian, so you're going the other way from heaven." If so, I was going to reply, "You know what? You're right. Fine."*[9]

I cried the first time I read those words. They still break my heart. Lance's issue is not with God; it is with his dad. But like any other normal person, if God even closely resembled what he had seen "Christians" like his stepfather model, then Lance wanted no part of it.

What about you? Have you ever thought about how your earthly father might have impacted your view of God? I can name certain areas where my father's imperfections caused me to have some less-than-accurate thinking about God. Even the best dad is not perfect; as a result, we all have some form of dad/God baggage. Here are some of the typical ways that dad images affect God's image:

- Dad died when we were young, so God is undependable.
- Dad was abusive, so God is harsh and judgmental.
- Dad yelled all the time, so God is angry.
- Dad was a workaholic, so God is unavailable.
- Dad ran off with another wife and kids, so God cannot be trusted.
- Dad was relationally challenged, so God does not really want a relationship with me.
- Dad was an agnostic, so God does not exist.

You get the picture. By the way, the reverse is true as well:

- Dad was a good provider, so God will provide.
- Dad was always there, so God is always with me.
- Dad was safe, so God will protect me.
- Dad was loving, so God loves me.
- Dad was faithful, so God will never betray me.

Does this help? Can you think of some ways your view of God may be hindered by your dad's own limitations? You don't have to be abandoned or abused to have dad baggage; we all have baggage to some degree. However, you can be sure that if you were abandoned or abused, or if your dad suddenly decided that he liked another family better than yours, or if you woke up one day when you were seven and found out that your daddy was never coming home because of a car wreck, you would be pretty inclined to not want to have anything to do with a God who could let you down like your dad did. Calling God "Father" would be unpalatable, to say the least...just ask the woman in my Sunday-school class.

Until we rethink God, until someone comes along and shows us a more accurate picture of who God really is, we are likely to continue to see him through the limited and imperfect filters of our earthly dads.

THE FATHER YOU HAVE ALWAYS WANTED

Enter Jesus. If you are looking for someone to offer an alternative view of the father concept of God, then look no further. Jesus deliberately and strategically linked God with the father image. He made no effort to shield God from all the possible father baggage that might be hurled his way. Jesus *wanted* us to see God as a father. He *wanted* us to rethink the father concept in light of who God is, and he wanted us to know God as our own father, just as he did.

In John's gospel, Jesus either directly or indirectly referred to God as *father* over one hundred times. It was by far Jesus' most frequently used metaphor for God. Baggage or not, Jesus was determined to introduce God as the Heavenly Father. His pictures of God are indeed attractive:

* *God is the father who desires intimate worship that is not tied to religious holy sites or bogged down in religious rhetoric.* (John 4:21–23)
* *God is the father who is the source of true life, and he freely dispenses it to any who believe in his Son.* (John 5:26)
* *God is the father who feeds all who are spiritually hungry with the eternal bread of Heaven.* (John 6:32)
* *God is the father who openly receives all who come to his Son.* (John 6:37)

- *God is the father who is a great shepherd; and the shepherd has ordered his Son to lay his life down for his sheep.* (John 10:17–18)
- *God is the father who promises to raise back to life all who believe in him.* (John 6:44)
- *God is the father who keeps all of his followers from being snatched away by the enemy.* (John 10:29–30)
- *God is the father who honors those who serve him.* (John 12:26)
- *God is the father who gives his spirit to those who follow him.* (John 14:16)
- *God is the father who gives us what we ask for in his name in prayer.* (John 16:23)
- *God is the father who takes his children safely to Heaven.* (John 17:24)

What do you think about such a God? Does he sound too good to be true? Does he sound like the classic, world-class, fictional dad? He is not, at least not according to Jesus. The God that Jesus proclaimed is a loving, perfect and real dad. He is the God you run to, not from, when you are in trouble. He is the God who wants to calm your fears, meet your needs, satisfy your hunger and quench your thirst. He wants to protect you from your enemies and answer your prayers. He wants to honor your service and obedience to him. And he wants to secure you and carry you safely into eternity. That is the God who Jesus believed in. That is the father who Jesus knew. And that is the God who Jesus invited us to worship. He is the real deal: *the Heavenly Father.*

Jesus knew the Old Testament—the Hebrew Bible—quite well. He was raised on its teachings. No doubt he was thinking of Isaiah's famous text (the one I was teaching to the group of seminary students) when he taught of God the Father: "For to us a child is born, to us a son is given, and the government will be on his shoulders. And he will be called Wonderful Counselor, Mighty God, Everlasting Father, Prince of Peace" (Isa. 9:6).

I love that powerful adjective in front of *Father—Everlasting.* Do you hear the promise in that? God is a father who will never get old and die. He will not lose interest in or grow bored with your relationship. He will never decide that you are not worth the effort. He is the Everlasting Father: the father who never lets you down, never disappears and never fails. I don't know about you, but that is the kind of father image I want...and need.

LIKE FATHER LIKE SON

I am sure by now you see a pattern developing. In Jesus' teachings, he was rarely content to talk about God in isolation. Inevitably Jesus would get around to talking about *his* relationship to God. Jesus did not claim to be one of many messengers of God. He did not argue that he was one of God's many children. The relationship with God that Jesus claimed was indeed unique; so unique in fact that his enemies sought to kill him because of his claims.

Consider this parenthetical statement by John: "For this reason the Jews tried all the harder to kill him; not only was he breaking the Sabbath, but he was even calling God his own Father, making himself equal with God" (John 5:18). What did Jesus mean when he claimed to be God's Son...and why did it make the Jewish leaders so angry?

There are many points that distinguish Christianity from other major religions, but Jesus' assertion of his divine sonship is clearly one of the weightiest. The significance of Jesus' claim to be God's Son was not lost on his Jewish audience. They clearly understood what he was saying. In Hebrew theology, God was unique and absolute. He alone was God, the creator and sustainer of all life. Good Hebrew thinkers had no room for multiple deities. They came by their monotheism naturally: God had made it very clear to them in the Ten Commandments that he alone was God and that worship of anything else would not be tolerated.

So the phrase "Son of God" created all types of interesting theological dilemmas for the Jews. God's Son was not a reproduction of God…there could not be a second little God. Such thinking violated the belief that God, indeed, was one. Thus, God's Son could only be one thing—God, in a human frame. God could only give birth to himself. He could not produce anything less than himself.

Any man brazen enough to claim to be God's Son had better know what can of worms he was opening. Claiming to be God's Son was not just saying you were like God or that you were another God; it was saying that you *were* God. And that, to quote the gatekeeper at OZ, was "a horse of a different color." The *Wonderful Counselor, Mighty God, Everlasting Father* and *Prince of Peace*, whose advent Isaiah predicted over seven hundred years earlier had, according to Jesus, arrived on the scene. He had been born under the mysterious circumstances associated with Mary, raised as a simple carpenter and was now an outspoken critic of the Jewish religious hierarchy. The Jewish leaders neither misrepresented nor misunderstood Jesus. They heard him correctly. Jesus was claiming to be their God. No wonder they wanted to kill him.

But Jesus was not being arrogant. He was not trying to push the Jewish leaders' theological buttons. In Jesus' mind, he was doing exactly what he was supposed to be doing: "Jesus gave them this answer: 'I tell you the truth, the Son can do nothing by himself; he can do only what he sees his Father doing, because whatever the Father does the Son also does'" (John 5:19). This was no fly-by-the-seat-of-your-pants ministry. Jesus was not making things up as he went. He claimed to be a very careful student of his father's activities. He claimed to imitate his father, even to the point of speaking only what he first heard his father saying. He claimed that his way was right and true, because it flowed naturally through him from God.

WILL THE REAL FATHER PLEASE STAND UP?

What conclusions, if any, should we draw about Jesus given his view of the fatherhood of God? It might be easy to first conclude that Jesus had a great relationship with his own earthly dad. That, however, is probably not the case.

Jesus may well have been a candidate for his own set of dad baggage. I am sure you are aware of the Bible's claims about Jesus' birth. Mary, the mother of Jesus, told the biblical chroniclers that she had given birth to God's Son as a virgin and that she never had sex with her husband Joseph until after Jesus was born. Jesus' enemies, if they were aware of the story, certainly gave it no credence. It was widely believed among Jesus' enemies that he was simply illegitimate—a point they were never hesitant to make (See John 8:41). Jesus no doubt grew up knowing the scandal that accompanied his birth. He knew that Joseph was his earthly father, but not his progenitor. As early as age twelve Jesus was referencing God as his father. That is some heavy-duty thinking for a preadolescent.

Beyond that, Joseph is never mentioned in the Bible after Jesus' childhood. Scholars are not sure what exactly happened. Most reason that Joseph died while Jesus was still fairly young. Regardless, it seems that Jesus did not grow up with the best of father situations. Joseph was certainly a godly and righteous man, but he could not totally shield Jesus from the rumors that must have been constantly circulating about his birth. Neither could Joseph prevent the pain that Jesus felt by losing him so early in life. In short, Jesus did not have a perfect father image from which to draw conclusions about God.

That makes his preferred use of the father metaphor for God even more astounding. Somehow, Jesus got the idea that God was the perfect dad. He may have drawn his conclusions from the Hebrew scriptures, for they certainly paint an attractive picture of a loving and benevolent, father-like God. Jesus knew enough Hebrew history to know God as the loving father and provider of Israel. But I believe there is more to it. Jesus' references to God as father seem so personal, so experiential. It is as if his understanding of God's nature was firsthand.

The Implications of Jesus' Teachings

What are we to make of Jesus' claims? How could a simple man, born in a remote village, in a nation occupied by a foreign power, uneducated and untrained, really believe that he was God's holy Son? On the surface, that sounds more like a story for the tabloids rather than Holy Writ, which is certainly an option. More than a few seekers in history have rejected Jesus solely on the rather audacious nature of his claims. The odds of one man being the actual and only Son of God are infinitesimal to say the least. And if he was, he surely could have done a better job of convincing his contemporaries that it was so.

From the human perspective, Jesus gets failing grades in the areas of marketing and career management. Couldn't God's Son have been a bit more convincing? Being crucified by the very people you claim to be king of does not read well on a résumé.

Thus, perhaps the easiest conclusion to reach is that Jesus was not the unique Son of God. He was well intended and kind, but certainly not divine. For many, their investigation of Jesus ends there and they move quickly on to the next stop in their search for truth.

But let's suppose for a moment that Jesus was indeed who he claimed to be. Now I am not asking too much here; billions of others in history have come to such a conclusion. For the sake of understanding, let's play the what-if game. What if Jesus was right? What if he was telling the truth? What if he was indeed God's Son? What would that say about God? What would that say about us? What are the implications for us if Jesus really was who he claimed to be? Let me list in simple fashion some of the conclusions we could then draw about God, Jesus and us:

- God really does exist, and his Son's advent proves it.
- God acted purposely in history to make himself known.
- God is innately good and benevolent.
- God came to us first, because there was no way for us to go to him.
- God sending his Son represents the greatest demonstration of love and sacrifice ever offered.
- Humans are inherently valuable to God and therefore worth his pursuit.
- Humans really needed saving—it is why God's Son came into the world.
- When Jesus' enemies rejected him, they were actually rejecting God.
- When Jesus' followers received him, they were actually receiving God.
- Jesus' claim that he was the only way to God is valid.
- Jesus' teachings on truth are therefore true.

There are many others, but I think you get the general idea. The conclusion that Jesus was God's Son doesn't leave us much wiggle room. If he was, then we must face the fact that God has set up the rules by which we must play the game. We do not get to pursue God on our own terms. If Jesus was God's Son, the system has been firmly established. We only get to choose whether to comply or not.

Given such narrow avenues within which we are asked to maneuver, it is easy to see why so many might choose not to. Having only one choice feels, to many, like having no choice at all. So they reject Christianity and Jesus altogether. A God, they think, who would require such strict compliance and offer so few options, must not really be worth pursuing. And so, their spiritual egos having been sufficiently bruised, they push on in search of a savior or religion that is not quite so restrictive of a human's free will.

But a true seeker must stop and ask the hard questions: Why would God create such an apparently flawed system? If God really is omniscient, then he surely must know that such a scandalously narrow path to him is bound to offend the independents and spiritual mavericks among us. If God really wanted to be discovered, then he would create many entrances into his heavenly home, not just one. Any good engineer knows that easy access always comes with multiple points of ingress. If God was smart enough to design the universe, why would he make the way to him so ridiculously narrow? That certainly flies in the face of all human logic.

And that may actually be the point.

If Jesus is God's Son, then God deliberately created such a narrow system. It might defy human logic, but it does not defy his. Either God was being purposely mean and elusive, or he knows something we do not. And if the latter is true, then perhaps we need to stop pushing away from God and instead start asking him what's up.

A MAN WHO TOLD US THE TRUTH

So what do you think? How has your relationship with your dad affected your view of God? You can be sure of this: we all form opinions about God based on what we see and experience in our dads. As a result, each one of us has an imperfect picture of God. In order for us to see God correctly and to know him more fully, we need an accurate picture. Jesus claimed to be that picture. He believed and taught that the best portrait of a loving father was God, and that he was the best portrait of God.

POINTS FOR PONDERING

Use as many adjectives as possible to describe your relationship with your dad.

Was your dad spiritual when you were growing up? If so, how serious was he about his faith?

Was his dad (your grandfather) religious? What kind of spiritual heritage did your dad inherit?

What kind of spiritual heritage did you inherit?

How do you think your dad image may have impacted your God image?

What do you think of Jesus' claims about God being the perfect dad?

What do you think of Jesus' claims to be God's unique Son?

What is your opinion today of Jesus Christ?

CHAPTER 5

And Deliver Us from What's-His-Name (The Truth about Evil)

• • •

JUST A FEW DAYS AGO, on the exact day I started editing this chapter, the twenty-seven-year-old copilot of a Germanwings flight locked the pilot out of the cockpit and then proceeded to calmly fly the plane into a mountain in the French Alps. His suicide flight also killed the 149 other people who were on the plane.

By the time you actually read this chapter, my guess is the Germanwings tragedy will be all but forgotten. Not that the story won't matter or won't still be terribly tragic; it's just that we can be quite certain that there will be new stories with equal or greater horror to attract our attention.

Whatever evil is, it seems to love to outdo itself.

Think about it—Oklahoma City, Rwanda, Al Qaeda, Bosnia, the KKK, Cambodia, Aurora, Sandy Hook, September 11, 2001, a Luby's in Killeen, Auschwitz, Oslo, ISIS, the Taj Mahal in Mumbai, Charles Manson, Charles Whitman, Hitler, the Boston Marathon, Virginia Tech, Columbine, Pan Am 103, an army barracks in Beirut, a train in London, an office in Paris and a subway in Japan.

Each of these names, places and dates bring to mind some kind of unspeakable horror—a kind of cruelty that still shocks us even though we have seen and heard it all before. If you live long enough and allow yourself to become calloused enough, you may conclude that such human behavior is, well, normal.

Normal might actually be easier to understand, because if you dare to call such behaviors *evil*, you have suddenly opened up an even greater can of worms. The concept of evil begs some very difficult questions: What is the source of evil? Who determines the standard for evil and its obvious counterpart, good? And can evil be controlled or even eliminated altogether?

According to a rapidly growing school of thought within neuroscience, evil is an antiquated and even harmful concept. What many of us call *evil* is really nothing more than a very small portion of the brain gone awry. Evil acts are nothing more than the inevitable results of bad wiring.

The implications of such thinking are obvious and are already being celebrated by many neuroscientists: there is no free will; those who commit "atrocities" are not ultimately responsible for their actions and are actually victims of their own neurological malfunctions. Immorality, and specifically evil, are no longer relevant concepts and no longer accurately describe the actions of those who commit harmful acts.[10]

Try telling that to the families of the 149 passengers on Germanwings 9525.

Just Give It More Time

Is there a source of evil, or is it really nothing more than unfortunate brain chemistry? Does evil really need no name or face associated with it? Is it really just an abstract reality in our society? How do we account for what we see? How do we explain it and come to terms with it?

I am not talking about the political and/or religious differences that generate murderous zealotry and hatred. While obviously wrong, they can be at least superficially accounted for by looking at the nature of their religious and/or political source. I am talking, rather, about the apparent degenerative condition of the human heart. The condition that somehow numbs a person to the reality and innate value of another person. The condition that makes inflicting immense pain and suffering on another not just justifiable but also enjoyable. What is it about humanity that enables us to have moments of brilliance and kindness on one hand and moments of unspeakable cruelty on the other?

Neuroscience notwithstanding, I would like you to wrestle with an important question: How do we account for the reality of evil in our world? Many place the blame squarely on God's shoulders. They want nothing to do with a deity who would condone, allow or in any way put up with such ongoing wickedness. To many, God certainly has the power to stop such madness. He obviously has not stopped the madness, and that is just too much for them to swallow. What good is a God who does not defend the innocent? What good is a God who tolerates mass murder, terrorism and genocide? God couldn't be all that great; otherwise he would not allow so much suffering. Such thinking is the party line for many in the anti-God crowd.

So how do we account for evil? We could claim it as a temporary negative trend in evolution, but that argument has obvious flaws. No such malevolence exists in the worlds of our would-be cousins. There is certainly violence, bloodshed and brutality in the animal world, but it is hard to find the animal equivalent of a mother strapping her two young boys into her car and sending it into a lake, a grandfather raping his granddaughter while her mother held her down or a husband murdering his wife and then claiming to be himself the victim of a violent crime. Such acts of sheer malice are unmatched by any of our nonhuman neighbors here on earth.

Evolutionists simply answer that as man's intellect and sophistication evolve, so does his capacity for good and/or evil. But therein lies the problem. How do we even know what good and evil are? Where did the standards for goodness and wickedness come from? How did we develop awareness of what aberrant behavior is if there exists no ultimate, nonaberrant reality? If we indeed have evolved in a material vacuum—with no outside spiritual influences—then why do we sense that anything is evil? How do we know it is evil? In an evolved material world, there is no moral standard by which good and evil are defined.

Is evil simply classic Darwinism at work? Surely evil cannot be seriously written off as the survival-of-the-fittest being played out in society. If that reasoning stands, then Hitler was not bad. He was, by that logic, simply a very efficient and effective expression of human natural selection. Few thinking people really believe that.

Either we don't really have the stomach for natural selection at work on the human level, or something else is going on. And if something else is indeed happening, then what is it? We are back to the families of the Germanwings copilot's victims, trying to put words to what could cause such a terribly selfish and harmful act.

How then do we account for this rather bad development in humans, and what, if anything, can we do about it?

Enter Jesus. As we have already seen, the teacher Jesus lacked no opinions on such socially relevant matters. As a self-described "man who told us the truth," Jesus believed that he had the inside track on all of the major questions and issues that plagued society. That certainly included the ultimate source and nature of evil.

Jesus didn't hesitate to not only give evil a name but also to describe its realm and its effects on the lives of men and women.

PERSONAL, MASCULINE AND SINGULAR

If you want to find out about a man's character, squeeze him. Put him in the vice of suffering and you will discover in a hurry what is really inside. Perhaps no greater vice has ever been devised than that which Jesus endured in the hours before his death. Betrayed by one follower and denied by another, and on his way to an unbelievably brutal and prolonged death, Jesus knew what it meant to be squeezed. What came out tells us much about his character. What came out was prayer, and specifically, prayer for others.

In the hours before his arrest, Jesus spent his time teaching and then praying for his followers. Jesus' prayer, overheard by John and subsequently recorded in his gospel, is the longest of Jesus' prayers in the Bible. It reveals much about his heart, his courage and his view of his mission. It also tells us what he thought about evil. In the prayer recorded in John's gospel, Jesus said, "My prayer is not that you take them out of the world but that you protect them from the evil one" (John 17:15).

This is certainly a curious statement from Jesus. He knew that he was only hours from death. He was asking God to give staying power and courage to his fledging group of followers. And yet the deliverance from evil that Jesus requested was not generic. He didn't ask God to shield his followers from evil conditions or from an evil in society. Jesus didn't even ask for protection from the evil Roman government that occupied his nation or from the arguably evil Jewish leaders who sought his death. No, the evil from which Jesus sought protection for his disciples was personal, masculine and singular—*the evil one.*

What a difference gender makes. Had Jesus chosen a neuter form of the adjective *evil*, we would be less likely to read a reference to a specific personality into his comment. But Jesus chose the masculine form of the word, causing translators to place the word *one* after *evil*. So here we have Jesus in a prayer to God, acknowledging the existence of an evil one and seeking God's protection from him for his disciples. Whatever Jesus thought of this evil being, he believed his followers needed protection from him and that such protection was best gained through prayer.

EVIL BY ANY OTHER NAME

You don't need a degree in advanced biblical studies to know that Jesus believed in the devil. The Jewish culture of which he was a part readily acknowledged the reality of the devil and demons, and the Hebrew scriptures he knew and studied taught of the same. Jesus, just by being a good Jew, believed in the devil.

But there was clearly more to it for Jesus. His take on the evil one did not seem limited to the Jewish understanding. As we have already seen, Jesus was in the habit of taking what the cultural and religious norms were on such topics as God and truth and either expanding them or redirecting them altogether. Jesus' teaching on evil was no exception. He offered unique insights into the nature of evil and he greatly advanced the theological thinking on Satan in his day. And he did so from what sounded like firsthand knowledge.

Jesus' descriptions of the devil reveal much about what he thought about him. Three times in John's gospel Jesus referred to the devil as the "prince of this world" (John 12:31; 14:30;

16:11). The phrase is more literally translated "the ruler of this world." Jesus not only believed in the devil but also believed that he had certain power and authority. The *world* to which Jesus referred was not the planet earth but rather the spiritual or invisible realm. Jesus believed in a well-organized spiritual system that was opposed to God. And he believed that system was led by the devil. Jesus knew nothing of the hoofed, pointed-tail, pitch-fork-carrying cartoon character that we see so frequently in media. He rather believed Satan to be a powerful, cunning and ruthless adversary, who commanded a vast array of wicked spiritual henchmen.

Jesus also believed that he himself was more powerful than the devil: "Now is the time for judgment on this world; now the prince of this world *will be driven out*...I will not speak with you much longer, for the prince of this world is coming. He has no hold on me... the prince of this *world now stands condemned*" (John 12:31; 14:30; 16:11; emphasis mine).

In each of these dramatic statements, Jesus referenced either the devil's impending judgment or his own power over him. Jesus said that the devil's demise would be accomplished when he (Jesus) completed the job that God had given him. Jesus believed that by going to the cross, he would, in fact, forever liberate the spiritual realm from the tyranny of the devil.

Once again we find ourselves standing on a uniquely high plain with Jesus. Religious leaders, prophets and scribes were certainly known to talk about and reflect on the wiles of the devil. Few, if any, however, ever dared to suggest that they could end his reign of terror. Jesus not only announced that he would beat the devil but he also said that he would do so through a most unlikely means—his sacrificial death.

Giving the Devil His Due

Jesus pulled no punches when it came to describing Satan. His hatred of the devil and his belief in the devil's inherent evil were obvious. In John 8:44, Jesus made a definitive theological statement about Satan's ultimate nature: "He was a murderer from the beginning, not holding to the truth, for there is no truth in him. When he lies, he speaks his native language, for he is a liar and the father of lies." Several points jump out from this statement about the devil that Jesus believed in.

Satan existed before material creation. Jesus' reference to "the beginning" no doubt speaks of the creation of the earth recorded in Genesis. Jesus obviously believed that Satan was a spiritual being that existed before humans were created.

Satan murders. Death and destruction are second nature to the devil. He cannot do good or be benevolent. He is violently opposed to anything of God and hates all who follow him.

Satan is a brilliant liar and the master of the evil spin. He lies about God and God's plan for people. He lies about what is right and wrong. He lies about humans, their origins and their value. He is the father of all fabrication.

He fights truth. Satan doesn't just lie…he openly opposes all truth. Truth, to Jesus, was the ultimate reality found in and defined by God. Satan refused to yield to such truth. He not only opposes God's truth but also seeks to recreate truth in his image with his lies.

He persuades human beings. This is a critical point, so don't miss it. In arguing for the existence of the devil, Jesus was in no way excusing people for their roles in sin. Humans are not innocent victims in the whole equation of evil. If a man murders, he must be held responsible for his choice to commit murder. But if a man murders, you can bet that he has been listening to a voice somewhere that was justifying murder for him. And that, said Jesus, is what Satan is so good at. He can lead a human to justify anything.

What do you think about Jesus' view of the devil? Does it seem too fantastic or supernatural to be real? It wasn't for Jesus. He believed in a spiritual world where two diametrically opposed forces were at war. He saw the devil as the archenemy of his father. He believed that he had been sent to expose Satan's lies and to ultimately strip him of all power. Jesus believed and taught that his work and obedience to God would forever condemn Satan and his wicked schemes. He also believed and taught that he had come to liberate those humans who had been taken spiritually captive by the devil. In other words, Jesus came to lead people out of the darkness.

NOT THE SMARTEST THING I'VE EVER DONE

In June of 2004, my then seventeen-year-old son and I climbed Mount Elbert, the tallest mountain in Colorado and the second tallest in the continental forty-eight states. At over 14,400 feet, Elbert is a big but friendly giant. The mountain's gentle slopes and lack of ledges and cliffs make it a popular and accessible climb. Many rookie hikers boast about having climbed the highest peak in Colorado, due in part to the mountain's rather easy approach.

My son and I did not consider ourselves to be rookie hikers. We probably were at that time, but we didn't think we were. I had climbed enough hard mountains in the previous thirty years to develop a rather secure opinion of my mountaineering skills. So the thought of climbing Elbert in the traffic of all sorts of hiking riffraff and wannabes bore no attraction to me at all. If I was going to summit the big dog mountain in Colorado, then it was going to be special.

So how do you take an easy climb and make it hard? How do you take an ordinary hike and make it unusual? How do you take a safe mountain and make it dangerous? (My wife would add, "How do you take a smart hike and make it stupid?") It's simple; you remove two basic safety features in hiking: light and heat. In other words, you climb the mountain *at night*. That's right; if you want to make an otherwise predictable climb unpredictable, just venture up an exposed mountainside at about 2:00 a.m. That will always do wonders for your excitement factor.

And that is exactly what we did. We left the safety and warmth of our truck at 9:00 p.m. and started up the trail through a thick, dense and animal-patrolled forest in the dark. The only light we had were the tiny beams that our cheap flashlights provided. The initial trail was steep and difficult, but in the dark, we couldn't tell how steep. It was easy to stumble and/or wander off the trail. Also, we knew we were not alone—we could just feel the wildlife watching us. Black bears and mountain lions own these forests. That is always great motivation to keep moving.

When we finally punched through timberline at about 11:00 p.m., we were greeted with an unbelievable sky. With no city lights to compete with the stars, we had a view of the heavens that I will never forget. The Milky Way seemed so close that we could just reach out and grab it. It really was spectacular. But with our new exposure and increased altitude came another not-so-welcome reality—cold. With no trees to insulate us, we found the temperature around us dropping dramatically. We had left the danger of animal attacks and now faced the ongoing discomfort of the cold, thin mountain air.

My son and I reached Elbert's summit at about 1:00 a.m. We couldn't see the unlimited view that the mountain offers. Our view was limited to just a few feet of the mountain's rugged top surrounded by the blackest darkness I had ever seen. It looked as if the darkness could just swallow you whole. It looked like a massive, unending black void. We paused on the summit only long enough to eat a quick snack and drink some water. But when we raised our water bottles to our now parched and cracked lips, nothing came out. The bottles were frozen. The water, even while being jostled around by our movements, and even while being kept in the relative warmth and insulation of our packs, had frozen solid. It was that cold.

We returned to the safety of the truck at about 5:00 a.m. Light was just beginning to form in the eastern sky. We had literally hiked all night. We checked the temperature at the truck. In the forest, at 5:00 a.m., at the relatively low altitude of ten thousand feet, it was thirty-two degrees Fahrenheit. It felt like a heat wave. We were shedding layers of clothes like we were in a desert. I don't know how cold it was on top of that mountain. I don't want to know.

In the mind of Jesus, the world of the devil is like a dark and lonely mountaintop. It is cold, it is black, and it can swallow you whole.

COME IN OUT OF THE DARK

There is a haunting scene recorded in chapter thirteen of John's gospel:

After he had said this, Jesus was troubled in spirit and testified, "I tell you the truth, one of you is going to betray me." His disciples stared at one another, at a loss to know which of them he meant. One of them, the disciple whom Jesus loved, was reclining next to him. Simon Peter motioned to this disciple and said,

"Ask him which one he means." Leaning back against Jesus, he asked him, "Lord, who is it?" Jesus answered, "It is the one to whom I will give this piece of bread when I have dipped it in the dish." Then, dipping the piece of bread, he gave it to Judas Iscariot, son of Simon. As soon as Judas took the bread, Satan entered into him. "What you are about to do, do quickly," Jesus told him, but no one at the meal understood why Jesus said this to him. Since Judas had charge of the money, some thought Jesus was telling him to buy what was needed for the Feast, or to give something to the poor. As soon as Judas had taken the bread, he went out. And it was night. (John 13:21–30)

Did you note that last sentence? *And it was night.* John's reference to *night* at the end of that passage is no mere allusion to the time of day. His term is as much a spiritual description as it is physical. He was communicating a theme that he had heard Jesus use repeatedly. Jesus offered the images of light and darkness to contrast his domain to the devil's and to distinguish the spiritual condition of those who accepted him from those who rejected him. For Jesus, Satan's realm was darkness. Men and women who did not follow God were themselves trapped in darkness. And whenever Satan is doing his evil work, there truly is the black darkness of night in the world. So when Judas went out at the bidding of the devil to betray Jesus, it was dark indeed.

Jesus saw a clear connection between evil and the darkness of the devil that shrouds human beings' souls. Evil actions were no bad human trait or temporary evolutionary breakdown. Evil was to Jesus the very evidence of a soul held captive. Humans do evil things, argued Jesus, because they are controlled by the ultimate source of evil. "You belong to your father, the devil, and you want to carry out your father's desire" (John 8:44).

Satan, according to Jesus, is very capable of swaying people's actions and controlling their desires. He can blind people to such a degree that what God calls evil actually begins to look good to them. He can skew the entire system of morality that God placed inherently within them.

In John 3, Jesus clearly linked evil actions to a person's preference for the devil's darkness. "This is the verdict: Light has come into the world, but men loved darkness instead of light because their deeds were evil. Everyone who does evil hates the light, and will not come into the light for fear that his deeds will be exposed" (John 3:19–20).

The light to which Jesus referred was his own life and ministry. His presence on earth was the same as a bright light being shown into a very dark place. It was heat and warmth in an otherwise cold and barren landscape. Jesus claimed that people rejected him because they disliked the light and accountability that he brought.

People in sin like darkness. It hides their actions and motives. Light offers no such safety. When a person in darkness is suddenly exposed to light, he either has to conform to the light or run back to the darkness.

While I was writing this chapter, a friend of mine revealed that he had a drug addiction. He had struggled off and on for years with a drug habit, and now, as a professional in his city and a leader in his church, he had an addiction that threatened to cost him everything. Over a series of very difficult days, my friend confessed his sin to his wife, to me and to other people in his life. He also started outpatient treatment and joined a group for men like him who were struggling with a drug habit. I call that "coming into the light." An amazing thing happened when this man started talking openly about his problem—he gained perspective. He was able to see in the lives of other men some of the same bad decisions that he was making. By seeing how their deception hurt their spouses, he was able to grasp how his lies hurt his own marriage. He was able to see that his problem was not unique…that other men just like him struggled with the same sin and had been able to overcome it. Walking in the light did wonders for my friend's recovery. Light will do that—it will either heal you or make you run.

Light always carries with it that choice. As the ultimate light-bearer, Jesus was a man who by nature drew lines in the sand. His truth-telling and light-shining caught many off guard. That is why, he claimed, so many people rejected him. They did not want the light that he brought, so they hid. When they found they could not escape the glare of his holiness, they tried to snuff it out altogether. They killed him.

Jesus made no bones about the fact that he saw himself as the solution to the world's problem with darkness. He claimed not only to be the one who would dethrone the devil but also to have the ability to liberate people from the stronghold of darkness. Jesus promised that those who turned to him would be protected from the power of the devil and his dark domain.

Consider John 8:12: "I am the light of the world. Whoever follows me will never walk in darkness, but will have the light of life." Or consider John 12:35: "You are going to have the light just a little while longer. Walk while you have the light, before darkness overtakes you. The man who walks in the dark does not know where he is going." And finally, listen to Jesus in John 12:46: "I have come into the world as a light, so that no one who believes in me should stay in darkness."

These comments in John's gospel are far too frequent and pointed to be viewed as merely illustrative. Jesus was not claiming to be a really bright spot on an otherwise really dark landscape. He was not just saying that he was an example of good in a dark and bad world. Jesus was not suggesting, as many claim, that he was simply showing us how to do away with evil by our collective goodness. Jesus, by his own words, seemed to think that only he was equipped to win the war with darkness.

WHAT TO DO WITH THE DEVIL?

What are we to make of this set of outrageous and unusual claims of Jesus? Here we have a man who not only refused to keep evil in the realm of the generic but also insisted on naming and personifying it. Jesus refused to settle for evil in the abstract. He argued instead for a wicked, personal reality that far surpassed our worst nightmares. Beyond that, Jesus said that the secret to overcoming this evil was not in education, social reform or individual and cultural evolution. He boldly declared that the only way the evil one would be vanquished was through his own brave and sacrificial actions.

Jesus, as if reading the mind of every imaginative Hollywood screenplay writer, told a story of an unbelievably wicked foe who held the world captive and was threatening to destroy it. And in perfect "the hero saves the day" imagery, Jesus said that he would save ours. Jesus claimed to be the only figure in history who could and would overthrow the powers of darkness. He said that he was the only hope for men, women, families and even nations that were held captive by the devil.

So what do you think? How do you respond to Jesus' explanation of evil? Is he too over the top, or is he genuinely onto something? Let's consider both sides.

First, let's suppose Jesus was wrong. Suppose that he was warped, deluded and way too interested in the whole evil-personified concept. Jesus did more to promote and advance the concept of Satan than any other religious teacher in history. So what are the implications on our understanding of evil if Jesus was wrong? Where does that leave us?

To begin with, we have to exclude any other supernatural explanation for evil. Remove Satan and his demonic hordes from the scene and we basically have to also rule out any other nonhuman influences. It would not make any sense to oppose the idea of a personified evil force just because Jesus said that one existed; neither would it make sense to theorize about another type of supernatural evil not reflected in Jesus' teachings. The results would still be the same. If Jesus was wrong, and the devil is only a myth, then we are one step closer to having to look in a mirror for ultimate answers about evil.

Second, we have to come up with a plausible, material explanation. Remove the reality of a devil and we greatly reduce the number of our explanations for evil. All that is left to us are things that we can touch, see and quantify. Without Satan, we have to struggle with a society that is innately capable of horrific acts. We are left with a race of humans gone terribly awry...or maybe not. Perhaps, without a devil to personify evil, questions about the nature and causes of evil will go away entirely. Perhaps we will simply conclude that humans who evolve in a solely material world just act that way and no higher level of behavior can be rightfully expected.

And finally, if Satan is not real, then we will have to admit that evil, whatever it may or may not be, is fully in control. Evolutionary theory suggests that given enough time, nature will fix whatever is wrong with itself. That being the case, either there is nothing wrong with what we consider evil or nature is incapable of fixing it. Evolutionists might respond that more time is simply needed for the true seeds of evil to be selected out, but such thinking seems rather superficial. Enough history has passed for the *de*volution of society to be painfully clear. Humanity and the problem of evil are not getting any better. Evil is, as history has shown, at least cyclical if not in fact getting worse.

In a world where humans are the ultimate evolved reality, we have to look squarely at ourselves for both the source and solution of such problems. And that is one rather depressing posture. For if people are the best there is, then we are clearly to blame for all that is wrong with the world, and as the millennia before us have proven, we are incapable of doing anything about it. If Jesus was wrong, then we need to adhere to the pagan philosophers quoted by the apostle Paul in the New Testament: "Let us eat and drink, for tomorrow we die" (1 Cor. 15:52).

THE JESUS SOLUTION

There is, however, the possibility that Jesus was right. As in the other areas of Jesus' teaching that we have discussed, the implications of Jesus' correctness on the issue of evil are as intriguing as they are radical. If Jesus was right, we have to rethink not only what is wrong with culture but also how it can be fixed.

If Jesus was right, then human beings are not the ultimate beings in the world. Open the door to supernatural evil and you open the door for spiritual realities and beings that go far beyond our ability to comprehend. If we are indeed being acted upon and influenced by outside sources, then we must come to the chilling conclusion that we are neither alone nor in control of our universe. If we acknowledge the possibility of an evil spiritual order, we must then also acknowledge the possibility of a good one, and not far behind comes the inevitable conclusion that the two are at war and that we are the ultimate prize.

If Jesus was right, then evolutionary thinking gets even foggier. Evolution offers a theory of the origin of material life. It has nothing to say about the origins of spiritual life. If humans are not the ultimate reality, and if there are forces we cannot control waging war over us, and if there are realities and beings in the universe that we cannot fully define or understand, then evolutionary thinking is in big trouble.

Evolution bets the farm on the material world being all there is. If Jesus was right and if we are suddenly confronted with the existence of a spiritual order that is not subject to time or physical laws, then evolutionists had better get to work on a theory that can account for such realities. And that may well prove to be a sticky wicket. Evolutionary theory has no good answer for the classic question of first cause—how the original speck of primordial matter actually came to exist. Or in the language of the big bang, who lit the first match? With the question of the original source of material existence remaining unanswered, one can only imagine the stress created for evolutionary thinkers when trying to answer the question of the source for a spiritual world.

If Jesus was telling the truth, then human beings are still faced with the ugly reality of our inability to overcome evil. If we are dealing with a devil and not just bad behavior, then at least from the human standpoint, the game is already up. Human beings, even with their collective creativity and intelligence, are no match for the evil being that Jesus described. We can't nuke him. We can't outlaw or legislate him. We can't reason with him or educate him into a higher level of sophistication. If Jesus was right, then we are dealing with a force that goes far beyond anything we have ever faced before. In short, we are at his mercy. Oh, and by the way, he has none.

If Jesus was right, then humanity really does need a Savior. Held captive by a tyrannical and ultimately evil foe, and trapped in the eternal cesspool created by their own sin and rebellion, humans are in big trouble. If rescue does not come through an outside source, a source that can not only overthrow the devil but also somehow atone for our sins, then rescue will not come at all.

No plot could be more dramatic, and this was exactly the scenario that Jesus described. In Jesus' mind, he was the Savior the world desperately needed. As God's holy Son, he had the power to defeat Satan. And as God's holy Son, he was the only one qualified to deal with the sins of humanity. Jesus believed that he had been sent into the world to expose the evil and lies of Satan. He believed that by dying in obedience to God's plan, he would actually disarm and forever condemn the devil. He also believed that he was the deliverer of a race of people condemned to an eternity of suffering because of their sin and Satan's schemes. In other words, Jesus not only believed that he had been sent to save the world but also that he was the only one who could pull it off.

A MAN WHO TOLD US THE TRUTH

The answers offered by Jesus are not easy ones. There are no easy answers when evil is the subject matter. But the answers proposed by Jesus are real nonetheless. He repeatedly stood before his colleagues and the religious leaders of his day and claimed not only to be their God but also to be their deliverer. Interestingly, the nation of Israel had for centuries been waiting for its deliverer to come. Hundreds of years of political oppression had caused the Israelites to long for rescue, and the promises of the prophets had told them to expect it. But the rescue they looked for was geopolitical, and the enemy to be defeated was Rome. They saw no need to wrestle with the bigger issues of sin and Satan. Perhaps they missed the point.

Have we? *Newsweek* religion writer Ken Woodward felt that he at least had to leave that possibility open:

> *Without a transcendent God, the Devil has no meaning and evil is just a metaphor for very bad luck...If the Devil has died to American culture perhaps it is because we no longer see in his myth the image of our own worst inclinations. But evil, if the Devil is to be believed, is more than personal sin. At times, evil so thoroughly triumphs in an individual, a society or a culture that it assumes a personality of its own. In moments like these, we can truly speak of the Devil.*[11]

POINTS FOR PONDERING

Imagine you were talking to a seven-year-old. How would you define evil?

If that same seven-year-old asked you about Satan, how would you answer?

Do you believe in a devil? Why or why not?

Do you believe in evil influences that go beyond human explanation? If so, what are they? Where do they come from?

What do you think of Jesus' claim to be the world's Savior? Do you believe him to be deluded, arrogant or greatly confused? Or are you open to the idea that he may have been who he claimed to be?

Do you think that the world needs saving?

Do you think that you need saving?

What is your opinion today of Jesus Christ?

CHAPTER 6

Betting the Farm on Love
(The Truth about Love)

• • •

THE SIGNIFICANCE OF LOVE IN the Christian faith is difficult to overstate. Jesus himself said that love was the true calling card of every Christian: "By this all men will know that you are my disciples, if you love one another" (John 13:35). Many, however, have questioned the wisdom of Jesus making such a claim.

Had Jesus wanted to really set his disciples up to win, wouldn't he have chosen a standard a little easier to achieve? How many people do you know who have written off Christianity because of its failure on this very point? The reputation of many in the church is that they do not love one another and they cannot get along...they fight, argue and even sue each other. Beyond that, many churches are known for what they hate and whom they oppose, not for what they support and whom they love. So when Jesus said that love was to be his disciples' bottom line, he set the bar way too high. Perhaps Jesus needed a speech writer to help him better plan his words. If he had just chosen another litmus test for true discipleship, then surely much of the angst about Christians could be reduced.

Suppose Jesus had said, *By this all men will know that you are my disciples, if you build really nice, expensive buildings in my name.* Case closed! No critic of the faith would have a leg to stand on. Christians have for centuries been the masters of grand and breathtaking architecture. But Jesus didn't say that.

Imagine Jesus had said, *By this all men will know that you are my disciples, if you create many specific rules and regulations to live by.* Once again, who could ever doubt? How many seekers of truth have been stung by the church's "Don't drink, don't dance, don't chew and don't date women who do" motto? If making rules had been the standard that Jesus set up for his followers, then they most certainly could have reached it.

What about theology? Had Jesus said, *By this all men will know that you are my disciples, if you become profound theological thinkers.* Had that been the case, the church would surely have few dissenters. The libraries and hard drives of the world can hardly contain all that has been written about Christian theological minutia.

I'm Not Feeling the Love

I could go on, but I'm sure you get the point. When Jesus chose the intangible, *hard-to-define-and-even-harder-to-do* standard of love as the birthmark of true believers, he seemed to have doomed his own work from the outset. Because of this very point—the expectation for love but the obvious lack of it among Christians—many cast aside Christianity.

Edward Boyd, a seventy-year-old agnostic expressed it well in the book, *Letters from a Skeptic*:

> *You invited me to raise whatever objections come to mind, so I'll jump right in. Here's one I've wondered about a lot: how could an*

all-powerful and all-loving God allow the church to do so much harm to humanity for so long? Isn't this supposed to be His true church, His representation on earth? That's what I was taught in my Catholic days. So I'm wondering, where was God when the Christians were slaughtering the Muslims and Jews—women and children included—during the "holy" crusades? Why did God allow "His people" to burn almost the entire population of Jewish "unbelievers" in Spain during the Spanish Inquisition? Why would an all-loving God allow the church to take part in something like the Holocaust (at best it looked in the other direction)—and do all these things "in His name"?[12]

In other words, "Where's the love?" Can you relate to Mr. Boyd's frustration? For an organization that is supposed to carry the banner of love, the church has done its share of woefully unloving things. Even with the potential of such failure, Jesus was adamant about the role of love in the lives of his followers. To him, it was the standout characteristic of Christianity. When Jesus wanted to narrow religious belief down to what God ultimately wants and expects from his worshipers, he came up with one verb—*love*. Win or lose, love was the bottom line for Jesus.

Now here is an obvious question: With so much potential for failure, why did Jesus insist on love as the litmus test for his followers' faith? And here is the answer: Because love was the primary characteristic of the God he proclaimed. For Jesus, it made perfect sense to set up love as the standard for authentic Christianity. In his mind, if people were genuinely connected to the God he knew firsthand, their love for each other would be obvious. Jesus could have picked another Christian calling card, but then he would have been untrue to his Father. Jesus called for love from his disciples because that is what he saw in his God.

WHAT THE WORLD NEEDS NOW

Lest we proceed with any confusion on this point, we need to define *love*. That is no easy task. But to keep things simple, let's look at the options that Jesus had for love. What did he mean when he said that love was the dog tag that would identify his disciples? To what love was he referring?

Well, we can start with what he did not mean. First, Jesus was not referring to anything sexual. The Greek word *eros* (our word *erotic* derives from this) was available to Jesus, but he didn't use it. Had Jesus meant sexual or romantic love, he surely would have said so. Second, Jesus didn't mean family or brotherly love. Neither was he describing strong friendship. Again, Jesus had words available to him that described such feelings, but none were his choice for love.

The word Jesus chose was the word *agape* (pronounced a-GA-pay), and it described the highest and purest love possible. Jesus used agape to describe his relationship to God. He used it to explain the interconnectedness between him as God's Son and God as his Father. Agape was how the Father and Son loved each other. It was, therefore, how their followers should love each other as well.

So what is this higher love that Jesus described? In short, it is lopsided love. It is love that does not make deals or seek conditions. It does not need prenuptials or contracts. It is committed love. So committed, in fact, that it is guaranteed regardless of the reciprocity factor. It is a love that will be there even if the recipient does not return it. It is unconditional, unmerited, unearned and unmeasured love. It is unjustified love.

LOVE OF ANOTHER KIND

In 1955, Martin Luther King Jr. led the black citizens of Montgomery, Alabama, in a boycott of the public transportation system. This famous and highly effective boycott was sparked by Rosa Parks' unwillingness to sit in the back of a city bus just because she was black. Dr. King rallied the black community and convinced them to stop using public transportation. Where reason had not prevailed, economics did. The financial impact of the boycott was so significant for the city that officials were forced to sit down and negotiate with Dr. King and other black community leaders.

This was no easy victory for Montgomery's black citizenry. Violence and threats of violence, destruction of property and even bombs were all used to try to get them to back down. Dr. King's strategy of nonviolent resistance was based on his understanding of Jesus' command to practice agape. In his book, *Stride Toward Freedom*, King wrote about his understanding of Jesus' meaning of love:

> *Agape means understanding, redeeming goodwill for all men. It is an overflowing love which is purely spontaneous, unmotivated, groundless and creative. It is not set in motion by any quality or function of its object. It is the love of God operating in the human heart.*
>
> *Agape does not begin by discriminating between worthy and unworthy people, or any qualities people possess. It begins by loving others for their sakes…Therefore, agape makes no distinction between friend and enemy; it is directed toward both.*
>
> *Agape is not a weak, passive love. It is love in action. Agape is love seeking to preserve and create community. It is insistence on community even when one seeks to break it. Agape is a willingness to sacrifice in the interest of mutuality. Agape is a willingness to go to any length to restore community. It doesn't stop at the first mile, but it goes the second mile to restore community…*

The cross (of Jesus) is the eternal expression of the length to which God will go in order to restore broken community.[13]

GOD POSITIVE

Did you catch the power of those descriptions? Have you ever heard of a more appealing form of love? The kind of love that Jesus required of his followers was the kind he saw modeled in his Father. It was the kind of love that a holy God would offer to an undeserving people. Jesus knew it to be what the world needed most. He also knew it to be impossible for any human to express such love without his Father's assistance. The love so eloquently described by Dr. King and required by Jesus is not a love that humans can manifest on their own. Agape, while normal on the divine level, is way beyond the reach of typical human behavior and feeling. It is supernatural love. It can never be naturally produced by fallible people, no matter how hard they try.

But when a person is rightly connected to God, when he is truly allowing God to live in and through him, then the *symptoms* of God will begin to show up in him. And for Jesus, the most obvious symptom or evidence of God was love. Show Jesus a person who is starting to spontaneously offer agape and he will show you a person who has been infected with God. That is why he set up love as the divine standard: those who are truly connected to his Father can't help but model it.

While agape may have lofty descriptions and definitions, its application is quite down-to-earth. For Jesus, the demonstration of agape in everyday life was simple. In fact, Jesus' expectations for agape in the lives of his followers can be summed up in two words. The first is *obedience*.

PROOF OF LOVE

Obedience to God was not a new concept for Jesus' audience. They knew quite well that, for God, love meant obedience. Young Hebrew children grew up reciting verses like Deuteronomy 10:12—"And now, O Israel, what does the Lord your God ask of you but to fear the Lord your God, to walk in all his ways, to love him, to serve the Lord your God with all your heart and with all your soul"— and Deuteronomy 11:1—"Love the Lord your God and keep his requirements, his decrees, his laws and his commands always."

Such commands made it clear that God took obedience seriously. He would not tolerate a people who boasted of their love for him but did not honor him with their actions. For God, obedience was the proof of love.

So Jesus' original audience was not surprised to hear him underscore the love-equals-obedience message. What did surprise them, however, was Jesus' command to obey *him*. That, said Jesus, was the same as honoring God. Furthermore, Jesus even said that the best evidence of a true love for God was obeying him (Jesus) and doing what he said. That, no doubt, thickened the plot for Jesus' followers.

Three of Jesus' statements in John's gospel reveal just how much he equated loving and obeying him with loving and obeying God. The first is John 14:15—"If you love me, you will obey what I command." Here Jesus pushed the envelope way beyond the typical teacher-disciple relationship. While teachers did instruct their followers, they did not typically give them commands. Jesus' language reveals much of how he saw himself and his followers. They were to love him and they were to obey what he commanded. Jesus obviously felt that he was worthy not only of their love but also of their submission.

In John 14:23–24, Jesus said: "If anyone loves me, he will obey my teaching. My Father will love him, and we will come to him and make our home with him. He who does not love me will not obey my teaching. These words you hear are not my own; they belong to the Father who sent me." Here Jesus stretched our view of his relationship to God even further. For Jesus, obedience to him invited God's love and presence into the disciple's life. God wanted to love and live with his people, and the conduit through which he made such fellowship possible was obedience to his Son.

Finally, in John 15:10, Jesus offered up the best example of the love he imagined: "If you obey my commands, you will remain in my love, just as I have obeyed my Father's commands and remain in his love." In calling for loving compliance, Jesus was not requiring anything of his disciples that he himself was not willing to do, and was in fact already doing. He simply said, *If you want to know what this agape thing looks like, just watch me.* The way Jesus honored and obeyed his father was the way he expected his disciples to honor and obey him.

What Does Loving Obedience Look Like?

"The world must learn that I love the Father and that I do exactly what my Father has commanded me" (John 14:31). Consider, for a moment, the obedience of Jesus:

- He was an obedient son, perfectly obeying his earthly parents.
- He stayed close to home and cared for his mother after his earthly father died.
- At age thirty, he was baptized publicly as an act of obedience and submission to God.

* He followed the difficult course of ministry laid out for him by God.
* He obeyed God by going to the cross.

The biblical writer Paul described Jesus' obedience in now-classic terms: "And being found in appearance as a man, he humbled himself and became obedient to death—even death on a cross" (Phil. 2:8).

For Jesus, obedience to God was quite simple: knowing what God wanted and then doing it. Jesus believed that God wanted him to die at the hands of the Jews and Romans. He also believed that by doing so he could forever communicate what true love looks like. Jesus did not hesitate to point to himself as the ultimate example of love. He challenged his followers to love like he did.

The love that Jesus proclaimed never weighs its rights or privileges. It does not consider what's in it for the giver of love. The love of Jesus is the ultimate others-centered posture. It is love exhausted, love emptied out, love spent and love spilt, all in the name of others.

Jesus told his followers that if they were to be true Christians, then they had to love each other like he loved them. Here are his own words: "My command is this: Love each other as I have loved you. Greater love has no one than this, that he lay down his life for his friends" (John 15:12–13).

Note that Jesus did not command his disciples to love *him* like he loved them. He did not ask for reciprocal love. Why not? Wouldn't Jesus have been justified in demanding such a return on his love investment? Maybe so, but to do so would have flown in the face of the very nature of agape. Remember, agape is unconditional, undeserved love. It never considers the possibility of a return. So Jesus told his followers to love *each other* that way—unconditionally.

But there was another reason Jesus did not require his followers to love him with agape love—they couldn't. The love shown by Jesus for his disciples was not peer-to-peer love. It was not love between equals. It was love between the divine and the human. When Jesus said that he loved and would die for humans, he was doing so as the Son of God. He never considered what he was doing as obligatory. He did not have to die for anyone. The love that Jesus showed for people was completely free. It was the ultimate no-strings-attached love. Jesus' followers could not love him the way he loved them—it was not humanly possible. They could not return the divine-to-human love, because they were human and Jesus was divine. So Jesus commanded them to love each other as he loved them. He commanded them to lay down their lives—figuratively and literally—for each other. That kind of love, said Jesus, would set them apart as his disciples.

Jesus told his disciples to obey him as he obeyed God. Their obedience to him would show up in sacrificial love for each other. This leads us to the second word that best describes Jesus' expectations of agape—*deference.*

AFTER YOU

To defer, in human terms, is to yield to another, to put oneself behind another, to wait upon another and to seek the best for another over and above one's own interests. Deference is the art of treating others like Jesus treated us. It is the ultimate *others-first* mind-set, even when the *others* are enemies. Deference is never done grudgingly or despairingly. It is always done in joy and out of love.

For Jesus, the best test to see if his disciples really got it was how they treated each other. He knew that if they really had his heart in them, then deferring would come naturally for them. Thirty years after Jesus' death, the biblical writer Paul wrote to a band of Christ-followers in the Roman colony of Philippi and reminded them of Jesus' call to defer: "Do nothing out of selfish ambition or vain conceit, but in humility consider others better than yourselves. Each of you should look not only to your own interests, but also to the interests of others. Your attitude should be the same as that of Christ Jesus…" (Phil. 2:3–5).

Such deference, in Jesus' mind, was where the rubber met the road in Christianity. Where agape prevailed, Christianity would be believable and credible. Where it faltered, so would the world's confidence in those who claimed to follow Christ.

Tragically, there are far too many examples of Christians who have missed it on agape. And while I am in no way trying to discount their incredibly negative impact in the world, these Christians' failures are not the whole story. There are plenty of examples, albeit rarely seen in the headlines, where followers of Jesus are doing exactly what he commanded. They love and defer to others like they are supposed to.

As a pastor, I have a ringside seat to these acts of love every day. I have been privileged to get to pass along the anonymous gift from one family who cares for another family in need. I have watched a husband and wife step in and fight for their good friends whose marriage was about to self-destruct. I have seen men pluck a Christian brother out of a life of addiction and walk him through the recovery process. I have witnessed average-income people give unbelievable amounts of money to alleviate the suffering of children half a world away. I have watched a group of Christian artists pool their resources to help send another artist to school. I have seen a heartbroken woman humble herself and forgive her adulterous husband…again. I have witnessed a group of single adults circle around and pray for one of their own who was suffering from a terrible physical illness. I have watched a group of Christians beg and plead with God to heal a man dying of cancer, and then rally to the side of the family when God chose not to. And, I have seen believers weep and dance for joy when CT scans that were once covered with cancerous spots came back inexplicably clear.

I have personally experienced levels of community and friendship that I could not dream possible. I have known what it feels like to be loved and forgiven unconditionally. And while I have never seen or been part of a perfect Christian community, I have had moments of joy and intimacy that must have resembled what Jesus called his disciples to model.

So, in spite of the headlines and cynicism that might suggest that Jesus' love standard is impossible, I would like you to consider the following people:

- Jeff, the physician who spends significant unpaid time doing medical missions in Central America
- Patty, who bought an inner-city building in Atlanta and converted it into a school for impoverished kids
- Tony, a former drug addict who helps current addicts, prostitutes and pimps get off drugs, get GEDs and become independent and productive adults
- The Johnson family, who cleaned up their neighbor's yard—a widow—after a damaging wind storm
- Danny, a computer-sales associate, who helped two younger colleagues in a different department, even though there was nothing in it for him
- Frank, a highly educated and capable former CPA, who runs a soup kitchen in a rough section of Boston

- James, the financial planner who has provided countless hours of assistance to Linda and her two young children after the tragic death of her husband
- The Burnell family members, who befriended and genuinely love the prostitute who lives next door
- Mary, married over forty years, who is guiding a much younger woman through the pain of recovering from her husband's infidelity
- Glen, a husband and father, who spent three weeks rebuilding homes in Grenada after it was devastated by a hurricane
- Members of the Walker family, who built an extra section onto their house so they could provide shelter for battered women
- Bob, who left a multimillion dollar business to become CFO of a nonprofit that builds orphanages in Africa
- Mark, a pastor, whose family took in a homosexual with AIDS and cared for him until he died
- Jill, who became a big sister to an inner-city child in Dallas and has encouraged, supported and modeled love for her through her college years
- Pete, who runs a home in Nashville that provides shelter, counseling, support and adoption services for unwed, pregnant teens
- Jim and Terri, whose specialty seems to be adopting babies born to drug-addicted girls and raising them in a loving and safe environment

None of these examples may stand out as particularly significant, and none of these people will ever be nominated for the

Nobel Peace Prize. They are refreshing examples, however, of Christ-followers who have taken quite seriously Jesus' command to love others with agape. And they give credence to the argument that the faith that Jesus started is the real thing.

A FUNNY THING HAPPENED ON THE WAY TO THE SYNAGOGUE

Marty was well over sixty years old when he started attending our church. He was a hard-driving, shrewd-in-business, rough-around-the-edges New York City Jew. Marty wasn't exactly practicing his Judaism. He was rather what you might call a cultural or social Jew, just like a cultural or social Christian. Marty did many of the external things that Judaism required, but his heart wasn't in it. In Marty's mind, God may have existed, but the two were not particularly on speaking terms.

Marty married a southern girl, moved to Austin and quickly established himself in the community. His business took off and he once again enjoyed levels of success similar to what he had experienced in New York. He also made several new friends, many of whom were Christians.

Over the years, Marty became more familiar with the Christian faith. Any defensiveness he might have originally felt around Christians eventually waned. Warm, genuine friendships were formed, and Marty was soon surrounded by a group of people who were trying to love each other as Jesus required. And to Marty's surprise, they began loving him that way too.

Soon Marty's heart softened toward the claims of Jesus Christ. After several months of seeking and theological inquiry, Marty knelt before God and yielded his life to Jesus. It was, and still is, one of the most beautiful life transformations I have ever witnessed.

I heard Marty tell the story of his pilgrimage to Christ on several occasions. One major theme was always there—love. Marty was apprehended not only by the love that he saw but also by the love that he received. He had never known a group of people to be so self-effacing. And he had never known a group of people to love him so freely. For him, the birthmark of love that Jesus said his children would have was clearly evident. Others-centered love—not good preaching, not great church architecture, not social or political reform—won Marty over. It was the most powerful argument for the validity of Jesus that he had ever seen. It was supposed to be. In John 17, Jesus prayed that his disciples would be unified as a sign of the Father's love. The results, he said, would be obvious: "May they be brought to complete unity to let the world know that you sent me and have loved them even as you have loved me" (John 17:23).

No Greater Love

So what do you think? Is it possible to see through the fog of centuries of cynicism and Christian failures and still believe in the kind of love that Jesus talked about? Is it possible for people to really love each other without condition? Was Jesus being overly optimistic, or can those who claim to follow him really love as he did?

It is really not difficult to explain the incongruities. Not all who claim to love Jesus really do. Many have embraced the Christian name with no real intention of ever honoring Jesus. Business, political pressures and social requirements have often driven people into the church who otherwise had no desire to be there.

Their failures in agape should not be surprising. They are trying to draw water from a dry well. But occasionally, stories surface about Christians who seem to get it right. Occasionally, you will hear about Christians who act, love, talk and give in such a manner as to make you wonder if Jesus himself were acting, loving, talking and giving through them. That was the kind of Christian calling card that Jesus was looking for. He wanted his disciples to love in such a way as to make people think of him. He wanted a love from his disciples that left absolutely no question as to its original source.

A TIME TO DIE

Consider Maximilian Kolbe, the "Angel of Auschwitz." Kolbe was born in Poland in 1894 and began studying for the Catholic priesthood in 1907, when he was just thirteen years old. He ministered during both World Wars, the second of which led him to begin using his monastery in Poland as a base for housing and supporting three thousand Polish refugees, two thousand of whom were Jews.

Kolbe, a committed Christ-follower, took Jesus' call to agape seriously. He and his fellow friars shared generously and liberally with the refugees. They exhausted themselves daily on behalf of those who were literally running for their lives. Inevitably, Kolbe and his associates fell under the suspicion of the Nazi SS. On February 17, 1941, Kolbe was arrested and taken to the Pawiak prison in Warsaw. Three months later, on May 28, 1941, he was transferred to the Nazi death camp, Auschwitz. Father Maximilian Kolbe, the servant of Polish and Jewish refugees, was issued the standard striped garment of an Auschwitz prisoner and tattooed with number 16670.

In camp, Kolbe was assigned the task of carrying logs. He continued his priestly ministry, albeit surreptitiously, by hearing confessions and offering Communion to his fellow prisoners. Kolbe was known to frequently give away his meager food rations.

Toward the end of July 1941, guards at the camp believed that an inmate had escaped from Kolbe's barracks. Nazis had a cruel way of dealing with escapees. Ten inmates were chosen from the escapee's barracks to die as punishment for the one who escaped. It was meant to discourage future escape attempts. On this day, Nazi guards selected ten men to die, unaware that the missing inmate actually lay dead in the latrine. There had been no escape, but the discovery would come too late to help these unfortunate men.

The ten men were to be led off to the notorious starvation bunker, where they would spend the next several days in an agonizing wait for death. One of the ten was a young Jewish sergeant, Francis Gajowniczek. Knowing that he would leave his wife and young children behind, he began to cry out for his family. And that is when the unheard of happened. Father Kolbe stepped forward and addressed the senior guard. He calmly explained that he wished to die in place of the young sergeant. When the guard asked who he was, Kolbe replied that he was a Catholic priest. He told the guard that he was old and that it would be more productive for the Germans to let the younger man live. The guard, unaccustomed to such acts of selflessness, acquiesced. Sergeant Francis Gajowniczek was returned to the ranks and Maximilian Kolbe took his place among the condemned.

That day, Father Kolbe and nine other prisoners were led off to Cell 18, the starvation bunker, where they were left to die. Intermittently, over the next several days, prayers and hymns could be heard coming from the cell.

After two weeks, four of the prisoners, including Father Kolbe, were still alive. They were taking too long to die! The bunker was needed for another group of victims, so the camp executioner was ordered to give the remaining prisoners lethal injections. Kolbe was the last to die. He is reported to have held up his emaciated arm in silent victory as he waited for the injection that would send him home. It was August 14, 1941; Father Maximilian Kolbe was forty-seven years old.

Francis Gajowniczek, the man Kolbe replaced, not only survived that day but also survived Auschwitz. He died fifty-three years later, on March 13, 1995, in Brzeg, Poland. He was ninety-five years old. Gajowniczek never forgot the man who died in his place, and he literally spent the rest of his life traveling the world and telling Father Kolbe's amazing and heroic story—a story of agape love.

Greater love has no one than this, that he lay down his life for his friends. (John 15:13)

LOVE OR BUST

Jesus Christ called his disciples to live selfless, others-centered lives. He said that such agape-based living would verify to the watching world that what he claimed about God was true. He bet the farm on his disciples' obedience to his Father and their love for each other. He bet the farm on love, knowing that many would fail.

Many more, however, have not failed. One of the reasons that the Christian church has survived two thousand years of intense scrutiny and opposition is because agape is happening. There have always been disciples of Jesus—and there are many today—who have obeyed his command to love each other as he loved them. They don't always make headlines, but they make enough of an impression to help countless skeptics find their way to faith in Jesus.

A Man Who Told Us the Truth

I am at the point in this journey where I must ask you to start personally considering the claims of Christ. I am ready to ask you to consider what sort of man would not only claim to be God's Son but also command men and women to love him and love each other in his name. I am ready to ask you to consider the various possibilities of who Jesus really was and the implications of each.

We are not finished with our journey yet, but we are at the stage where you need to consider where it might be taking you.

Points for Pondering

Have you ever known people who modeled unconditional love? Who were they and how did they model it?

Do you personally know Christians whom you would consider to be failures at agape? Do you personally know Christians whom you would consider to be genuine models of agape? What, in your mind, is the difference between the two?

What do you think of Jesus' equating loving and obeying him with loving and obeying God? What does that tell you about Jesus' sense of identity? What do you really think about it?

How are you on the agape scale? Do you love people without expectation of payback? Do you think you need to be more selfless in your love?

What, right now, is your opinion of Jesus Christ?

CHAPTER 7

Heaven's Chauffeur
(The Truth about Death and Heaven)

• • •

THE FIRST TIME I MET Mark Ayotte (pronounced *EYE-it*), he was sitting on his back porch. It was the day after his wife, Karin, passed away.

Karin had been attending our church for several months. Karin was quiet but friendly, and she had recently become involved with a women's Bible study in our church. I didn't know Karin well—just enough to greet her and know her name. And I did not know at the time that she was pregnant. What I did know was that she was at church frequently and seemed to be profiting from her time with the other Christian ladies.

Then, on one Wednesday night during church, I got word that one of our members was in critical condition in an area hospital. She was having emergency surgery and might not survive. It was Karin. She had given birth to healthy twin baby girls four days earlier. But on that Wednesday, Karin woke up in unbelievable pain. She was rushed to the hospital, where they quickly discovered that a blood clot had broken loose in Karin's leg and was making its way toward her heart. After many unsuccessful attempts to either thin or stop the clot, doctors decided that surgery was the only way to save her life.

As soon as our church service was over, I found a member of Karin's small group and asked if she had any news. Her look told me everything: Karin had died in surgery. She was twenty-nine years old, the mother of a four-year-old girl, four-day-old twins and the wife of a man who rarely attended church. That night, as soon as I got home, I called that man and asked if I could meet him the next day. And that is when I met Mark—on his back porch… in the shock and numbness of suddenly losing his wife…waking up as a thirty-year-old widower with three little girls and having no relationship with God. At the time, Mark would have described himself as an agnostic.

What happened over the next several years was truly amazing. Mark, to his credit, did not disappear from the church. Many of the people in our church who had known Karin reached out to him. He received several offers for help with his girls, who were now the three most popular children in Austin. Mark may have been mad at God, but his anger never turned hostile. Both of Mark's parents had died in their forties, and Karin's death seemed like just another bad event in a long line of bad events in Mark's life. But Mark saw that church was good for his girls, and even if he was not particularly interested in our faith, he kept coming for their sakes.

Mark and I became friends. We were not the socializing kind of friends, but our relationship clearly went beyond the typical pastor/church-attendee boundaries. We shared an affinity for classic rock 'n' roll, and often joked about him being the only person in our church who was constantly asking for the music to be *louder*. Mark and I made it a point to get together every few months for lunch. I would check up on him and the girls and ask where he was on the whole God thing. Mark's exposure to our church and to so many Christians eventually began to have an effect on him. Over the years, Mark's heart softened toward Jesus. And on August 8, 1999, I stood in the waters of Lake Austin and baptized my friend Mark Ayotte. I remember slamming Mark down into the water and making a huge splash. Mark's was not a particularly gentle baptism. I wanted to make sure that it took.

Later, long after he became a Christ-follower, I asked Mark at one of our lunches about his decision to follow Christ. I wanted to know what the biggest determining factor had been for him. Mark's answer floored me. That day, over a Thundercloud Subs at the Arboretum in Austin, Mark shared something with me that few people knew. He told me that after Karin died, he really wanted to throw in the towel on all religion. God had taken away the three people closest to him. He just didn't seem like a God worth pursuing. But something had happened on the day Karin died that Mark could not get over.

After several long hours of waiting with little information about Karin, the doctors told Mark that Karin needed emergency surgery. They said that Karin was very critical and that she might not live. Mark was told that he could see Karin for just a few minutes before they took her away. Mark remembered that Karin was relatively coherent and alert. She asked about the twins and their older daughter. Mark assured her that they were fine. Mark then asked Karin if she knew how critical she was and if the doctors had told her that she might not live. They had. Karin and Mark were both aware that this might be their last conversation.

Mark told me that there was something about Karin in their brief minutes together that he could not figure out. There was an amazing calm about her. Mark actually called it "peace." Karin had been in tremendous pain all day, but her exhaustion and suffering was not what Mark noticed. Describing his final moments with Karin, Mark wrote: "The only thing that I clearly remember from those last moments before they wheeled her away was the look in her eyes. 'Unbelievably peaceful' is the only way that I could describe it. This is the first thing that I have ever experienced that I could not explain or understand using logic. She should have been scared, but what I witnessed was anything but that."

As I sat there at lunch with Mark that day, he told me that whenever he got to the point in his pain and frustration where he was ready to let go of any hope that God was real, he always drifted back to those final moments with Karin. The otherworldly nature of what he saw in her eyes and his own inability to explain it kept him open to the possibility of God. Eventually that possibility would win him over.

In the midst of Mark's spiritual struggle, he experienced a strange but familiar feeling. He said: "Then at my lowest point, I had another experience that I couldn't explain. I was sitting on my bed, crying uncontrollably, not knowing how I was going to survive another day, when I decided to give prayer a try. I prayed for help, and all of a sudden, I realized that I felt really good. Peaceful. Peaceful like I had never felt before. Peaceful like that look that I saw in my wife's eyes. I immediately handed over control of my life to Christ."

Mark's story has a happy ending. His sister and brother-in-law moved to Austin from San Diego to be with Mark after Karin died. Mark ended up meeting a lovely woman at our church and eventually married her. Today, Mark and his wife, Linda, and the three girls are a very happy family. They love God and love serving him together. They still attend one of our church campuses, and Mark is the volunteer local missions leader for the congregation.

And to think it all started when Mark was watching his wife die.

WE'RE NOT TOO SURE ABOUT GOD, BUT HEAVEN SOUNDS GREAT

While God still plays to mixed reviews in US popularity polls, Heaven is actually doing quite well. Not only do most Americans believe in Heaven, but most also expect to go there after death. Obedience to and a clear understanding of God notwithstanding, Heaven is thought to be the next stop on the tour of life for most Westerners.

So what is Heaven? What is this ethereal, cosmic place that so many of us believe in? What is Heaven, and what does it have to do with eternal life? Are the two different, or one and the same?

What is Heaven? Will I know it when I'm there, or will I sit in Heaven and wonder about Heaven?

What is Heaven? Will I enjoy it? Are there really harps, clouds, streets of gold and angels with halos?

But the ultimate question seems to be: What is Heaven, and can its promise really make death bearable? Is Heaven, or the hope of Heaven, what gave Karin Ayotte such grace in her final moments? Can the reality of Heaven really negate death's sting?

Death, it seems, is what stands between the spirit and Heaven. Death is the point of entry, the rite of passage required for all who would seek entrance to the divine place. And that, for many, is a real problem. While most of us are excited about Heaven, few of us want to go through death to get there.

Peter Kreeft, professor of philosophy at Boston College, suggested that it might be worth the trip: "Heaven is the greatest good. It is the reason that God banged out the Big Bang eighteen billion years ago. Next to the idea of God, the idea of Heaven is the greatest idea that has ever entered into the heart of man, woman or child."[14]

If Heaven is indeed the best idea next to God, then it might well be worth the pangs of death required upon entrance. But is

Heaven all it's cracked up to be? Could Heaven actually be a bummer? Is it possible to get to Heaven and feel shortchanged? I mean, wouldn't all of that harp-strumming and cloud-sitting get old?

Religion writer David Van Biema seemed to dismiss such an idea as ludicrous. He sounded almost biblical when he described Heaven in a *Time* article: "Heaven is destination and reward, succor and relief from earthly trials. It is reunion with those we love, forever, as we loved them. It is our real home, our permanent address, our own true country. It is the New Jerusalem and Paradise Regained, the community of the Saints and the eternal Eucharist; everlasting Easter and a million Christmases. It is an end to death's sting; it is the eternal, ongoing, ever-growing experience of God. It is the ecstatic dream of St. John, 'Holy, holy, holy.'"[15]

That actually sounds pretty good, doesn't it? Sign me up.

A Room with a View

Jesus, the world's most influential religious leader, talked at length about Heaven. That should come as no surprise. Neither is it surprising that he had rather unconventional things to say about Heaven. By now you have probably figured out that whatever was a major theological emphasis in religion, Jesus was going to somehow connect himself to it. Heaven was no exception. Jesus affirmed the idea of a spiritual place where God's people would spend eternity. But Jesus went much further with his view of Heaven. To Jesus, Heaven was being with him. It was unencumbered fellowship and interaction with him in the realm where he was most at home—God's unrestricted presence.

In the hours before his arrest, Jesus gave some important final instructions to his remaining disciples. The teaching is found in John, chapters 13–16, and it is known among Bible scholars as the

Farewell Discourse. In it, Jesus used the promise of Heaven to comfort his followers in the face of all that was to come. He said: "Do not let your hearts be troubled. Trust in God; trust also in me. In my Father's house are many rooms; if it were not so, I would have told you. I am going there to prepare a place for you. And if I go and prepare a place for you, I will come back and take you to be with me that you also may be where I am" (John 14:1–3).

This is one of the most popular and frequently used biblical texts at funerals, and it is easy to see why. Let me sum up what Jesus said here about Heaven:

* It is real; it really does exist.
* Its reality should help keep our hearts from being troubled.
* It is the place where his Father (God) lives; it is his Father's house.
* It is large and roomy, and it has many individual rooms for guests. You will never find a *No Vacancy* sign out front.
* Jesus is Heaven's advance man; he is there right now getting your room ready for your special arrival.
* Jesus is Heaven's chauffeur. When it is time, he will come and personally escort you to your new home.
* Jesus is Heaven's main attraction. Heaven, to Jesus, is all about getting to be with him on his home turf.
* You can believe everything that Jesus says about Heaven, because trusting him is the same as trusting God.

Intrigued? If I walked up to you and started boasting about my access to and rank in such places as the White House, NASA's mission control, or the strategic defense bunkers buried in the hills outside of Colorado Springs, you would probably think that I had fallen off my bike a few times too many. Well, that is basically what Jesus did; only the place he claimed to have access to was none other than God's living room.

We need to be careful not to write off Jesus' comments about a place specially designed for each of his disciples as a sweet but unrealistic Hallmark notion. For in that quaint metaphor about Heaven there may well be hidden a profound theological reality. It sounds as if Jesus was revealing something about the nature of Heaven *and* the nature of our spirits. Was Jesus suggesting that Heaven is not just a place that we *get* to be, rather a place that we are *supposed* to be? Was Jesus suggesting that Heaven is really where God has intended us to be all along? Was he suggesting that we were actually made *for* Heaven? Perhaps, just perhaps, there is more to Heaven than harps and clouds. Perhaps, Heaven is about the very fulfillment of our soul's deepest longings.

C. S. Lewis, the British atheist-turned-Christian who became a popular Christian writer in the mid-1900s, commented on Jesus' description of Heaven: "Your soul has a curious shape because it is a hollow made to fit a particular swelling in the infinite contours of the divine substance, or a key to unlock one of the doors in the house with many mansions. For it is not humanity in the abstract that is to be saved, but you—you the individual reader...Your place in Heaven will seem to be made for you and you alone, because you were made for it."[16]

In other words, not only are you incomplete without Heaven, but Heaven also is equally incomplete without you. So much so that not only did God send his Son to die for the sins that would keep you out of Heaven, but when you believe in Jesus, and when it is time for your life in Heaven to begin, God will also send Jesus to earth to personally collect your living soul and see you safely to his Father's house. Jesus wanted his followers to live—and die—with their eyes on Heaven. He wanted them to be hopeful because there was a room there with their name on the door.

THE DIFFERENCE BETWEEN EXISTING AND LIVING

We have already seen on multiple occasions that Jesus liked to redefine important theological concepts. Well, in matters of life, death and Heaven, he may have outdone himself.

Jesus obviously believed in the spiritual realm—a dimension where God, the devil, angels and demons, and the disembodied spirit of every person, ultimately reside. He also believed that the spiritual realm controlled and affected the material/physical realm. What was ultimately real, for Jesus, was that which was spiritual. Time, space, matter—these were all finite and temporary realities to Jesus. But things spiritual, things invisible, things intangible, things not subject to time or the laws of physics—these were the stuff of ultimate existence. Jesus believed and taught that the spirit would outlast the body and that death was a transition, not an end. Jesus also taught that true life—life as he knew it—was that which existed on the spiritual plain. A person could be alive physically but dead in spirit, and a person could die physically and still be very much alive spiritually.

You see, life to Jesus was not defined by a successful seventy- to eighty-year span of uninterrupted heartbeats. That was what Jesus called existence, not life. Life, for Jesus, was determined by one's connection to God. Physical existence—that beating-heart reality—is guaranteed to every person to some degree. We all live on earth for a time—some long, some tragically short. It is simple physical existence. It is life, but only on the physical plain. It is standard factory issue from God—every human soul exists because God made it.

Spiritual life, or as Jesus called it, eternal life, is a different thing entirely. It is not guaranteed to every person; it is not standard factory issue. It is given only to those who have a relationship with God and have had their sin-damaged spirits repaired by him. Every person is born as spiritually damaged goods because of the spiritual disease of sin. You can be alive physically (drawing breath, beating heart, eating, drinking, procreating, etc.) and still be dead spiritually. Jesus offered his followers *life*—not just physical existence, but eternal life, spiritual life, through the removal of the guilt of their sins and the rebirth of their spirits.

John quoted a conversation between Jesus and a well-known religious leader that has been both misquoted and misunderstood for centuries. I am sure you have heard it. The conversation went like this (see John 3:1–7):

> RELIGIOUS LEADER: Teacher, we know you are a teacher who has come from God. For no one could perform the miraculous signs you are doing if God were not with him.
> JESUS: I tell you the truth, no one can see the kingdom of God unless he is born again.
> RELIGIOUS LEADER: How can a man be born when he is old? Surely he cannot enter a second time into his mother's womb to be born!
> JESUS: I tell you the truth, no one can enter the kingdom of God unless he is born of water and the Spirit. Flesh gives birth to flesh, but the Spirit gives birth to spirit. You should not be surprised at my saying, "You must be born again."

Jesus' trademark "You must be born again" statement reflects his belief in the difference between physical and spiritual life.

Physical life, given at human birth, is what each of us has by nature. Spiritual life is given at the second birth, or when a person is born again. It comes by invitation only—yours. In other words, you must ask for it.

Now here is the point of all this: for Jesus, while Heaven and eternal life are very connected, they are not the same. Eternal life begins the moment a person's sins are forgiven and he or she becomes connected to God. That can happen when a person is age seven, seventeen, forty-seven, one hundred and seven, or anything in between. When an individual becomes rightly related to God, their eternal life begins immediately, at that instant. The person's spirit will never again be in danger of spiritual death. It will live forever. It will, however, transition from the captivity and limitations of the human body to the freedom and spiritual bliss of an eternal one. That transition happens at death. And at death, the spirit of a person finally finds its way home. It arrives under Jesus' care at the place prepared for it by Jesus himself. It settles into God's eternal dwelling in Heaven, it finds its ultimate fulfillment in God's eternal presence and it rests in God's eternal security. A spirit at home with God will never hunger or thirst, feel pain or know fear, grow old or get sick, or experience anything other than unhindered intimacy with the all-powerful and holy God of the universe. That, to Jesus, was eternal life. And that, to Jesus, was what Heaven was for.

And in case you missed it, Jesus claimed to make it all possible.

Do You Think My Life Insurance Company Will Pay Twice?

Jesus was quite bold when discussing his connection to eternal life. He basically argued that he was its source and its meaning. In John

5:24, Jesus said, "I tell you the truth, whoever hears my word and believes him who sent me has eternal life and will not be condemned; he has crossed over from death to life." Believing Jesus' message was, to him, the same as believing the message of the one who sent him—God himself. Jesus had no problem asserting that listening to and following him secured one's place in eternity and protected one from the condemnation of sin.

John reported that Jesus demonstrated his power over death by raising his good friend Lazarus from the dead. Lazarus had been dead for over three days, well past the time when the Jews believed the spirit separated from the body and death's physical decay had begun. Before Jesus called him back to life, Jesus said to Martha, Lazarus' sister, "I am the resurrection and the life. He who believes in me will live, even though he dies; and whoever lives and believes in me will never die" (John 11:25–26). Jesus told this grieving woman that the life he offered was not subject to the laws of physical death. He argued that the life he offered actually trumps death. It conquers death, it supersedes death, it goes on regardless of death and it even gets better after death.

John reported that Jesus actually wept before he raised Lazarus from the dead. Why would Jesus do that? Why would he cry before restoring life to his dead friend? I think it was because he regretted having to take Lazarus out of Heaven. Lazarus was home. He knew what it was to have no pain. He had seen God. Jesus was saddened because he knew that not only did Lazarus have to leave Heaven, but he would also have to die all over again to get back there.

Imagine the conversation between Jesus and Lazarus, after Lazarus was raised, when Jesus was trying to explain to his close friend why he had plucked him out of paradise and dropped him back into the middle of a hostile, sin-filled, sickness-infested, evil world, to be relentlessly doted over by two well-meaning but annoying sisters, only to have to die again. You try explaining that to a friend. It's enough to make anybody cry.

THE CURE FOR THE COMMON DEATH

Just so you don't miss the point, Jesus' claims to be the source of eternal life were not isolated. He made enough statements about giving life and shutting out death to make his audience fully aware that he had a serious God-complex. Only it was not a complex. Jesus really believed he had power over death. Imagine being in the audience and hearing Jesus say, "I tell you the truth, if anyone keeps my word, he will never see death" (John 8:51). What kind of man did Jesus think he was? Who in the world thought that his words could actually cancel out death? Only God can do that. Exactly.

Or imagine hearing Jesus say: "For my Father's will is that everyone who looks to the Son and believes in him shall have eternal life, and I will raise him up at the last day" (John 6:40). I can see more than a few of Jesus' good Jewish audience members doing a serious double take on that one. They knew what "the last day" meant. The "last day" was the Day of Judgment prophesied about throughout the Hebrew scripture. It was the day when God would raise the dead and separate the good from the evil, the believers from the unbelievers, and send some off to eternal judgment and others to eternal life. It was God's day of reckoning with the world. What sort of man said that he would not only be around on the last day but also be the one raising up the believers? Nobody dared to say such things. But Jesus did.

And finally, so you will know that Jesus' talk about his being the source of eternal life was not just for the crowds; in his final prayer to God before his arrest, Jesus offered his definitive statement on eternal life. He said, "Now this is eternal life: that they may know you, the only true God, and Jesus Christ, whom you have sent" (John 17:3). It is one thing to boast before an adoring audience that you have got death mastered and quite another to pray it to God when only your inner circle of disciples is listening. If Jesus was bluffing on the whole *I can conquer death* thing, then the time to come clean was *before* the guards came to arrest him for blasphemy. He didn't. Even in his final moments of freedom, Jesus prayed that the eternal life he knew, the fellowship with God that he experienced and the eternal radiance that he bore would be clearly visible to all who believed in him. He prayed for every Christian to get to Heaven so that they could know and experience what he had. He actually prayed that we could see his eternal glory: "Father, I want those you have given me to be with me where I am, and to see my glory, the glory you have given me because you loved me before the creation of the world" (John 17:24).

Press Time

What do you think when you hear Jesus talk like that? What kind of man really talks to God like that in his prayers? Our cynicism quickly responds, "Only a loon." Maybe, but Jesus certainly didn't act loony. So what do you do with a man who claims to have power over death? What do you do with a man who claims to be able to provide eternal life, spiritual existence, and have access to the very dwelling place of God? And what do you do with a man who says that he can take you with him to Heaven, that he is preparing a place for you there and that you belong there with him? What do you do with a man like that? What kind of man would say such things?

I am ready to ask you a hard question. Let me ask it, press you just a bit and then I will back off for a while: What makes you so sure that Jesus isn't the real deal? In the face of so many over-the-top statements, you have to begin to wonder about him, don't you? Surely you know that if Jesus' disciples and the early leaders in Christianity were going to fabricate a story about a mythical messiah, they certainly would not have put such ridiculous claims in his mouth. They were too smart for that. No one on the religious landscape in Jesus' day was talking about overcoming sin and death. They were talking about overcoming the Roman Empire. No one was preaching about spiritual kingdoms. The kingdom that needed restoring was the Kingdom of David, along with the glory days of Israel. No group of religious zealots would ever dream up such an outrageous religious figure as the one Jesus appears to be in the New Testament. And that, at least to me, makes Jesus all the more alluring.

HOLY GROUND

Well, let's conclude this chapter by returning to the concepts of death and Heaven. Jesus taught that death was not to be feared. He taught that it was the gateway to real life. Jesus actually prayed that his followers might be delivered through death to Heaven, so that they could fully know life. And Jesus promised that when it came time for them to die, at the precise moment when every one of his followers was facing the dark front door of death, he would be right there with them. He promised to come and get them—in the hospital bed, at the nursing home, in the martyr's cell, on the executioner's scaffold, in the wreckage and debris, whatever the source and wherever the event of death—at the moment when their room was ready.

On March 6, 1997, my mother was hit by a severe case of septicemia. If you are not familiar with it, septicemia is a serious poisoning of the blood that results when toxins from an infection seep into the blood stream. Septicemia ravages the body and usually kills its victims, regardless of their age or relative health.

My mother was sixty-five at the time she got sick. She should have died. Her kidneys both failed, and she had a mini-stroke and a heart attack, all in the first twelve hours. I remember asking the ICU doctor which part of my mom's condition he was most worried about. He tersely replied, "Pick an organ."

But my mother surprised all of us, and she somehow survived her initial bout with septicemia. After three months in the hospital, she graduated to an assisted-living facility, where she would start learning how to live again.

You see, my mom was left very weakened by the septicemia. She was alive and spunky, but her body had really been through it. One kidney never started working again, and the other only worked at about 25 percent capacity. As a result, my mom had to endure kidney dialysis four hours a day, twice a week.

On two separate occasions, we brought in hospice to help my mother die. We were told that she simply could not live in such a weakened state. But my mother continued to defy the odds. On both of those occasions the hospice workers ended up "firing" her because she refused to die. We used to joke about having an "I Survived Hospice...Twice" T-shirt made for her.

But in January of 2011, my mother's body finally began shutting down. My birthday is January 6, and I knew that would be the last one I spent with her. Six days later, on January 12, we huddled around her bedside throughout the day and tried to seize the brief moments of alertness that my mother had in her final hours. At about 10:00 p.m., she slipped into a coma, and then the dreaded, telltale death rattle showed up in my mom's breathing.

My sisters and I kept vigil by her bedside throughout the night. Her breaths got slower and slower as the night lingered on. She went from breathing twenty times a minute down to ten, and then down to only five. We were literally counting her breaths—exhale, inhale, exhale…inhale, exhale…inhale, exhale…inhale. We watched and marked every last one of them.

At 6:30 a.m., I checked my mom's pulse. I couldn't find one. We knew she was close. Then, at 6:35 a.m., on Thursday, January 13, 2011, it happened. What I am about to describe only took about two seconds to transpire, but it seemed as if it were in slow motion. I certainly remember it in slow motion. It happened with my two sisters and I all sitting right there on my mother's bed, just a few feet from her. Since that day, on multiple occasions, we have replayed and confirmed what each of us saw. This was not a dream or a collective hallucination…what I am about to describe is what we all actually witnessed.

Besides her labored breathing, my mother had shown no signs of life since about 10:00 p.m. She had not moved, opened her eyes or looked alive in any way. At 6:35 a.m., she coughed. Then, in one simultaneous series of acts, her eyes opened and appeared very bright and alive, she smiled, and she sat up straight in her bed.

I need to explain what I mean: My mother had no strength. She had not eaten in weeks and was very emaciated. She could not even lift her hand to hold a paper cup filled with ice chips. When I say she sat up, she did not use her arms to prop herself and wiggle her way up. And she did not bend at her waist and lean forward. She led with her chest, with her head, shoulders and arms following behind. It was almost as if someone had grabbed her gown right at her sternum and had pulled her suddenly and forcefully up into a sitting position.

The bright eyes, the smile and the forceful sit-up happened right after the cough. She remained in that pose, eyes ablaze with life, only for an instant, and then her body fell back into the bed. She was gone.

My sisters and I knew immediately what we had seen. We had watched my mother leave. It was stunning. Seventy-seven years and three hundred forty-one days after God delivered my mother into this world, he had escorted her out. It was my sisters' and my honor to witness it.

When a Christian dies, Jesus comes to get him or her. Jesus promised to come and personally take us to the heavenly home he has prepared for us. Jesus is our own personal escort into Heaven. And I was there when he landed, ever so briefly, in my mother's room and took her spirit with him. It was holy ground.

Only Jesus can do that. Only Jesus can take a room marked by the pallor of death and turn it into holy ground. I am just glad I was there to see it.

A MAN WHO TOLD US THE TRUTH

On the day when your room is ready, on the day when your heart will beat its last and you will breathe no more, on the day when your physical life will end, he will come to get you. If you believe in and follow him, you will not leave this place alone. The Lord Jesus will come again and receive you to himself so that where he is, there you can be also.

I have to tell you: I don't fear that. I honestly cannot wait for the day.

When Mark Ayotte was spending his final few minutes with his wife Karin, he encountered a force that he had never experienced before. He called it peace. In reality, peace was only a piece of evidence or a sign of what Mark was sensing. Karin Ayotte was a Christian, and she was dying. Over two thousand years earlier, Jesus Christ, a man who told us the truth, promised to come get Karin when she died. He kept his promise. What Mark experienced was not just peace; he experienced the Prince of peace. He was on holy ground. Jesus had come to get Karin. Mark was experiencing Jesus. No wonder it changed him.

POINTS FOR PONDERING

Do you believe in a spiritual realm? Do you believe in a higher reality than what we can see or measure?

Do you think that you have a soul? If so, what happens to your soul when you die?

Are you afraid of dying? Why or why not?

Do you believe in Heaven? Why or why not? If you do believe in Heaven, what determines whether or not you get there?

What do you think of Jesus' claims to be the source of eternal life?

What is your opinion today of Jesus Christ?

CHAPTER 8

False Summits
(The Truth about Religion)

• • •

Say the name Smithsonian, and you probably think of the amazing series of museums in our nation's capital that literally display history before our eyes. You might also think of a great institution dedicated to mining the past. But that, actually, is only part of the story. Did you know that the largest budget on the Smithsonian's well-financed ledger is dedicated to the realm of exploration, specifically space exploration? As far back as 1838, when the whole notion of the Smithsonian was still being debated, John Quincy Adams proposed that government monies be used for an astronomical observatory. He called it a "lighthouse in the skies."

The Smithsonian Astrophysical Observatory (SAO) is our government's answer to Adams's lighthouse. Boasting over nine hundred researchers, staff members and students, and a partnership with Harvard University in the Harvard-Smithsonian Center for Astrophysics, with giant submillimeter-wavelength antennae in Arizona, Chile, Hawaii, Massachusetts, the South Pole and outer space, the SAO is in the business of "probing the universe for the unimaginable."

The observatory, according to Secretary of the Smithsonian Lawrence Small, "brings unsurpassed breath to the study of the universe." It studies "how the universe behaves" and keeps its multibillion-dollar eyes and ears trained upward in the never-ending search for clues to "the deepest secrets of nature," and for any indication that there just might be life out there that we have yet to discover. Small concludes, "Human beings have always had good reason to be humbled when they look to the heavens, and better reason not to be deterred [from our search]."[17]

Ladies and gentlemen, welcome to religion. No, I am not suggesting that the scientific search of the heavens is the same as humanity's search for God, but I am suggesting that the two are related. For as we humans probe the universe for its boundaries, its laws and its behaviors, we can't help but wonder if we might somehow stumble onto the answer of how it all got here to begin with. In other words, exploring the deepest secrets of the universe is not a merely material exercise. Too much remains unknown about nature, humans, life and our origins to say that our search only has material implications. Say what you will about the mechanics of how things happened *after* the beginning, few theories have much to offer about the moments *before* the beginning, and to go there is to knock on the unpopular door of the supernatural, if not the spiritual. Theologians, by the way, have for centuries labeled that same door "religion."

Is Anybody Out There?

Why do religions exist? When defined not as people's adherence to a set of faith-based behaviors, but rather as people's search for and/or belief in God, religion is a curious phenomenon. What makes so many in the world think that something beyond them is out there? Why have so many in history labored for, written about, prayed to and even gone to war in the name of this higher force? What is it about our world that makes us believe in God? Or, perhaps better stated, what is it about *us* that makes us believe in God?

Go to your favorite search engine, type in "religion," and be ready to stay there a while. Next to sex, religion and philosophy may be human beings' most popular stopping points for consideration and musing. Countless forms of religious expression—Christian, Eastern, pagan, New Age, metaphysical, Native American, along with countless variations of these—dot our cultural landscapes today. Why is that? Is it because something is obviously there to be found? Does the existence of religion—humans searching for God—confirm the reality of the God for whom we search? Does not this perceived hunger and thirst in humans imply that there is indeed something out there that can truly satisfy those cravings?

Many scientists today reason that religion is part of a "God gene" that has simply evolved in humans. That would be the ultimate irony: God really is a figment of our own evolved imaginations. But why would we imagine something beyond ourselves? Why would evolution produce something that is not in response to a legitimate need? In evolution, nature does not waste time creating new species or traits within species that do not meet obvious, recognizable needs. Natural selection responds to outside stimuli and produces life that is better equipped to survive in its environment. Why (or how) would religion evolve if there was not an outside stimulus for it, namely God?

Whatever your take on them, you have to acknowledge that religions in our world are plentiful indeed. Humans, right or wrong, are for the most part convinced that we are not alone in our existence. And because of that innate belief in something more, we search. It is that search, that pursuit of God by humans, that we call religion.

And it is in that search, that religious pursuit of God, that Jesus said we would never find him.

ENTER AT YOUR OWN RISK

Jesus was not a fan of religion. In fact, he reserved his harshest criticisms for the religious elite who seemed to call spiritual seekers to lifestyles and practices that were not only impossible to live up to but also meaningless before God. According to Jesus, God was not impressed by religion.

Now perhaps you are already confused. Perhaps you are wondering how one of the best-known "religious" leaders in history could be so hard on religion. And how could someone who founded such a significant "religious" movement as Christianity be so openly opposed to religious movements? Isn't that a bit hypocritical? Not if we don't put words in Jesus' mouth. You see, Jesus never claimed to be a religious leader, and he never claimed to be founding a religion.

Religions, according to Jesus, were the work of humans. They were evidence of people's search for God. Christianity was neither. The faith that Jesus launched was to him a work of God—it was God-initiated, God-sponsored, God-dependent, God-centered and God-targeted. It was God's work from start to finish. To Jesus, Christianity was nothing like the religions that were and still are so plentiful in the world's cultures. To categorize Christianity as such, according to Jesus, was to miss the point entirely.

I need to offer you a slight word of warning here: The stakes are about to get much higher. So far, we have seen Jesus take typical areas of theology and either expound on them or redirect them. We have seen him deal with love, evil, Heaven, God and truth in rather unique fashion. But there still appears to be some common ground or overlap between what Jesus said and what many spiritual seekers in the world today consider to be true. Jesus has so far been radical, but not *that* radical. That is about to change.

In the remainder of this chapter and in the next, our study of Jesus is going to take us into uncharted spiritual waters. Because Jesus, ever the intrepid prophet, is going to say even more things that no other spiritual leader was willing to say. We will see that Jesus rewrote not only the definition of religion but also the definition of God. Jesus is going to stand before the religious leaders and spiritual inquirers of his day and boldly claim to be the spiritual line of demarcation in all of history.

Here is my word of warning: Jesus asserted that his message was ultimate truth. He claimed that it was inspired, that it offered true spiritual illumination and that all who heard it were accountable for it. He said that his truth was the greatest news ever given to humanity, as well as the most important. It is information, said Jesus, that calls for a response. So if you keep reading, and I encourage you to do so, know that what you discover about Jesus may, in fact, stir your soul more than you are used to. You might just find yourself being drawn in ways that you haven't before. You might feel a holy nudge to decide, to respond, to react and to adjust your life to what you are discovering. You might just determine that Jesus was a man who told us the truth.

THE DIFFERENCE BETWEEN RELIGION AND CHRISTIANITY, PART 1

Jesus really did believe that he offered something different. He did not view himself as yet another religious teacher in a long line of religious teachers. Jesus never claimed to be just another cog in the wheel of human beings' religious journey to God. When considered as a whole, Jesus' teachings about himself and the nature of the faith he authored really do distinguish themselves from the realm of classic religions. Jesus' words are too *self*-centered and *self*-promoting to be classified as religious dogma. He did not talk about what spiritual seekers needed to do nearly as much as he talked about what he was doing. He did not offer instruction for religious behavior nearly as much as he called men and women to follow him. And he totally negated human beings' ability to get to God on their own. Jesus did not believe that spiritually inquisitive people, when left to themselves, could find their way home. He argued that the entire seeking process depended on God.

Listen to his words: "No one can come to me unless the Father who sent me draws him, and I will raise him up at the last day" (John 6:44). He went on to say: "This is why I told you that no one can come to me unless the Father has enabled him" (John 6:65). Now remember, we are talking about a man who claimed to be truth personified, who claimed to know and be God, who redefined love, who claimed power over the devil and who said that he was the only way to Heaven. Added to that, he claimed that even the attraction to him that human beings feel is God-initiated. Jesus had no confidence in the spiritual discernment of humans. He was convinced that even spiritually minded people, left to their own insights, would always stray off course and thus never find God. He believed that their spiritual homing-devices were broken because of sin, and only through the instruction he offered, mingled with the divine wooing of God, could a seeker find that which he sought.

That certainly flies in the face of what religions teach. Religions are all about going and doing. Classic religious teaching says: *Here is what you need to do: Go here, pray this, behave this way, learn these tenets, achieve this standard of morality, make these sacrifices, and then heaven/divinity/nirvana/paradise (or whatever the particular religion sets up as its goal) will be yours.* Jesus offered no such formulas. He taught that people are spiritually unable to accurately discern the way to God. He asserted that people have to be drawn, enabled by God, to even know to look for him. In other words, if God did not woo, if he did not stimulate the spiritual yearnings within each of us, then we would not know to search for him in the first place.

The faith system that Jesus presented was entirely dependent upon God. And that, for the control freaks among us, is a difficult pill to swallow.

We are at a critical stage in our discussion, so we need to drill down a bit further on what Jesus claimed the differences were between religions and Christianity. As you will see, these differences represent why Christianity appears to be so narrow and exclusive. Take a look at the diagram below. It is a picture of the approach of religions to God.

Please note several things about the world's religions.

Religions originate with humans. In every major world religion, the point of initiative is with people. Humans wake up and decide that there is more to reality than they can see. So they seek, they pursue and they look for what might be out there. Religions dictate to their respective adherents what needs to be done, what steps need to be taken and what courses must be followed. But in every case, the process originates within us. We recognize the need and we set out to meet it.

Religions are numerous and greatly varied. Few religions offer the same formulas for achieving their stated goals. The approaches to God that they offer are as numerous and different as the religions themselves. Some require strict adherence to a set of moral principles, some call for self-improvement through introspection and personal discipline and others seek spiritual perfection gained through a series of well-lived and upwardly advancing lives (reincarnation). The courses laid out in our world's religions are not uniform. They are highly distinct and vary greatly from one another.

Religions have different goals and differing ultimate objectives. Those who claim that all religions ultimately lead to the same place (and there are plenty today who do) have not done their homework. The call today for a synchronistic approach to faith is as naïve as it is uninformed. Religions today do not agree on what the end goals are. They do not claim the same endpoints for humans and they do not recognize the same ultimate outcomes. Religions offer everything from eternal bliss, where your every carnal and fleshly desires are fulfilled, to a static condition of spiritual perfection, to ultimate unity with the universe and every other "created" thing, to you actually becoming a god and ruling over your own world.

The paths of religions differ because their ultimate desti-
nations differ. There is no agreement between the major world
religions on what humanity is aiming at. That is, I think, why
religions are in fact so popular. Not only can the spiritual seeker
determine the outcome he wants, but he can also determine the
price he is willing to pay to get there...much like a spiritual version of Priceline or Expedia.

Religions always fall short of reaching God. This, quite obviously,
is not something that the world's religious leaders would agree
with. It was, however, precisely the point that Jesus was making.
His *No one can come to me unless the Father who sent me draws him*
statement rules out any potential for success on the part of people
when it comes to reaching God. Regardless of the nobility of our
religious aims or the selflessness of our religious efforts, Jesus asserted that we always fall short of reaching God.

This is not to say that God does not want to be reached. Jesus
was not suggesting that God was somehow playing a sickly divine
version of hard-to-get. We have already seen that Jesus knew God
to be the perfect Father, that the God of Jesus was both good and
giving. So what, then, is so wrong with our religions? Why would
Jesus so completely discount them?

Simply put, they miss the point. Religions simply fail to address what is broken in humankind. Our greatest need—the forgiveness and removal of sin—is not something a religion can meet.
In other words, the problem is beyond our ability to solve. Were
religions able to repair the rift between God and humanity, there
would be no need for Jesus to come into the world and die for sin.
But the severity of the solution that Christianity offers reflects the
severity of the problem that it has diagnosed. Humans are incapable of saving themselves. They need saving, and by a source not
of their own making.

THE DIFFERENCE BETWEEN RELIGION AND CHRISTIANITY, PART 2

Now, consider the following diagram of Christianity:

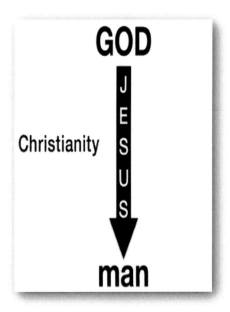

Let's look at some of the unique points Jesus claimed about Christianity.

Jesus claimed that Christianity begins with God, not people. Note in the diagram that the point of origin is with God, not humans. Christianity has nothing to do with human beings' efforts to find God; it has everything to do with God's efforts to reach humans. In the Christian faith, God saw our need for deliverance from sin and took matters into his own hands, quite literally, by becoming man and coming to earth.

Jesus claimed that in Christianity, the goal is singular and very clear. There are few options for people along the path that Jesus laid out. God initiates the process, and God himself is the goal.

Unlike the buffet offered by religions, Christianity is very narrow. The way to God goes squarely through faith in Jesus himself, and the ultimate goal is eternal life with God in his holy presence. The apparent rigidity and selectivity of this approach has been a point of offense for spiritual seekers for centuries. Our independent nature wants to push back against such limiting of our freedom of choice. It also begs the question about the fate of all who somehow are not fortunate enough to stumble upon the correct trailhead that leads to God.

What happens to those people in history—those who lived before Jesus and those who never hear of him—who do not have access to the way of Christ? What happens to good and well-intending people who are immersed from birth in one of those religions that Jesus discounted? These are good questions, and we will deal with them in the last chapter. Suffice it to say that the answers were not troubling enough to keep Jesus' original followers from embracing his message and proclaiming him as the only way to God.

Jesus claimed that in Christianity, God became man. This is clearly the most distinctive point in the Christian faith. Note in the graph that the arrow begins with God and descends all the way down to man. That arrow represents the descent of God. It represents what is known in theological terms as the Incarnation. It is the Advent we celebrate at Christmas.

Jesus claimed that in his efforts to redeem humankind, God did not send a substitute, a representative or a mere messenger. He did not drop down the formula for salvation on golden tablets from Heaven. Rather, he became the message: he himself dropped down from Heaven. He himself was the formula for salvation. There is no more personal offering of hope and deliverance in any religion in the world. In Christianity, the creating and holy God of the universe set aside the rights and privileges of deity so that he might condescend. This great condescension was his once-and-for-all solution to the greatest problem of human-kind—sin. This great condescension had in mind a very clear objective—our redemption. And this great condescension was made visible and available in history by the life, death and resur-rection of one man—Jesus.

COME ON DOWN!

Jesus left no room for doubt concerning what he thought about his origins and his mission. Twelve times in his gospel, John quotes Jesus talking about how he *came* from God or *came* to earth. It is not the language of someone who thinks he arrived here in the usual way. Look at some of his following statements:

- *This is the verdict: Light has come into the world, but men loved darkness instead of light because their deeds were evil* (John 3:19). We have already seen that Jesus viewed the darkness of people's souls as the work of Satan and that he viewed his role as the light that illumines the truth of God. In this verse, Jesus claimed to be the Light of God that came into the world.
- *For I have come down from heaven not to do my will but to do the will of him who sent me* (John 6:38). Not only did Jesus claim to have come from Heaven, but he also claimed to have been sent directly by God to accomplish his purposes.
- *Jesus said to them: "If God were your Father, you would love me, for I came from God and now am here. I have not come on my own; but he sent me"* (John 8:42). Jesus believed that he

and God were so inseparably linked that to love one was to love the other. He stated that he came to make the Father's love accessible.

* *For judgment I have come into this world, so that the blind will see and those who see will become blind* (John 9:39). Jesus was sent by God into the world to expose religious hypocrisy and judge those who misled people in God's name.

* *The thief comes only to steal and kill and destroy; I have come that they may have life, and have it to the full* (John 10:10). Don't misinterpret Jesus' apparent casual reference to a thief. In this verse, Jesus was contrasting himself and his work to Satan. Jesus came to give life to all who would follow him, and he promised to give it to the fullest degree possible.

* *If I had not come and spoken to them, they would not be guilty of sin. Now, however, they have no excuse for their sin* (John 15:22). Jesus stated that he came to raise our level of accountability before God. He said that those to whom he is revealed, those who hear his message, have no excuse for not following God.

* *No, the Father himself loves you because you have loved me and have believed that I came from God. I came from the Father and entered the world; now I am leaving the world and going back to the Father* (John 16:27–28). This is perhaps one of the most "why Christianity is not a religion" statements by Jesus. He clearly asserted that he came from God to share God's love, and when his work was completed, he would return to God. He basically said that his role in history was to make the way to God clearly known to all people. He said that God sent him specifically for that purpose. And because

of his unique origins, he claimed that only the path laid out by him was valid. Note: no other religious leader ever made such audacious claims.

Jesus viewed his life on earth as no mere accident. He did not consider himself to be one of the masses who walked the earth in random existence. Jesus believed and claimed to have been *sent* here. He claimed to have come from Heaven with the precise purpose of connecting people to God. He believed that he could do for people what they could not do for themselves. He claimed that if he did not complete his work, and if people did not follow the way to God prescribed by him, then only judgment and condemnation was left for them.

At this point you may have begun to see why Christianity is so scandalous and offensive to so many. Perhaps you have a better understanding of why Jesus refused to leave the door open for the validity of other religions and why his followers stick by their theological guns so adamantly.

Jesus, right or wrong, did not see himself as an alternative or his proposed path to be a really good option for many. He made no such generous overtures and we should not try to force any upon him. Jesus claimed to be the bearer of the way to God. He claimed to know what others did not, to have seen what others had not and to have been where others could not go. He basically said that in the search for God, people had two options: they could go the way of humanity (religions), never find God and end up fatigued and frustrated by their efforts, or they could go his way (through faith in him) and actually be found by God. There is not really much room for negotiation there, and that is exactly how Jesus wanted it.

THE TRUTH SHALL SET YOU FREE

I noted in the first chapter that Jesus offered "freedom" through his message of truth. Perhaps now we can begin to see exactly what type of freedom Jesus was describing.

Jesus was extremely critical of the organized religious movements of his day. He saw them as tyrannical and burdensome. The three other gospel writers (Matthew, Mark and Luke) each recorded severe statements Jesus made against the religious hypocrisy and legalism that he witnessed. Matthew even recorded a long series of "Woe to you" statements in which Jesus flatly condemned the elite religious leaders and said that God did as well. Jesus viewed much of the religious dogma of his day as people's attempts to control other people's behaviors and as empty-hearted expressions of an even emptier faith. The multiple prayers, rules, fasts and instructions that accompanied much of his culture's religion did not impress him.

That, quite honestly, is what has drawn many worn-out religious followers to Jesus. For centuries people who seemed unable to "make the cut" in their respective religious fields have found Jesus' teachings both refreshing and liberating. Those who previously felt bound and condemned in an impossibly rigid system of religious score-keeping found freedom and life in the relationship with God that Jesus described. Jesus himself claimed to have already done the works required by religions. He does not require his followers to meet God's holy standards, but rather to simply embrace that which he has done on their behalf.

Could this be the freedom that Jesus was talking about? Could it be that, through faith in Jesus, we are free to come to God as we are and not be required to jump through religious hoops to impress him? Is it wishful thinking to believe in a God who does not have some type of spiritual checklist? Is it wishful thinking to believe that God really would accept us as we are, even in our sin and guilt? Not according to Jesus. He offered freedom from the religious tyranny of his day. He came to set captives free from systems of religious performance that not only failed to impress God but also failed to address the original problem that existed between God and humanity.

FREEDOM FROM RELIGIOUS GUILT

Martin Luther was born in Eisleben, Germany, in 1483. He was the son of a Saxon miner and had originally planned to become a lawyer. But one day in 1505, Luther was caught in a thunderstorm and nearly struck by a bolt of lightning. The terrified Luther prayed for deliverance to St. Anne, the patroness of miners in Catholicism, and promised to become a monk if she saved him from the storm. The storm passed and Luther kept his vow. Two weeks later, Luther entered the Augustinian monastery in Erfurt and became a very dedicated monk.

Luther's ministry as a monk had its dark side. He was obsessed with guilt. He was terrified of God and overwhelmed by his own sinfulness. No amount of penance or religious rigor was enough to appease Luther's troubled soul. He worked feverishly around the monastery. He prayed for hours on end, frequently fasted, kept long vigils and read profusely. He would often deny himself sleep or sleep without a blanket in the winter in an attempt to decrease his own personal comfort. Luther later joked that if it were possible to get to Heaven by "sheer monkery," he certainly would have.

The weary priest sought refuge in the pages of scripture. He accepted an assignment as the Chair of Biblical Studies at the University of Wittenberg and gave himself to the thorough study of the New Testament. He was fascinated by Jesus' cry from the cross, "My God, my God, why have you forsaken me?" Luther couldn't understand why God would forsake Jesus, a man never guilty of sin. Perhaps, Luther began to reason, it had to do with Christ's own willing association with the sins of humanity. Had Jesus really died for sinners? Had Jesus really died for *him*?

Finally, in 1515, Martin Luther found the freedom his soul so desperately needed. While studying the book of Romans, Luther got stuck on Paul's words, "For in the gospel a righteousness from God is revealed, a righteousness that is by faith from first to last, just as it is written: 'The righteous will live by faith'" (Rom. 1:17). It was as if he was seeing a part of God he had never seen before.

Luther commented: "Night and day I pondered until I saw the connection between the justice of God and the statement that 'the just shall live by his faith.' Then I grasped that the justice of God is that righteousness by which through grace and sheer mercy God justifies us through faith. Thereupon I felt myself to be reborn and to have gone through open doors into paradise."[18]

Luther had found something that his over-the-top religious efforts could never offer—freedom from his guilt. He came to believe that he was justified before God by his faith in the work of Jesus, not by his own zealous efforts.

Luther's understanding of God's grace radically changed his view of God and of his relationship to him. A heart that had previously cowered in fear before God now sought him with open passion. So changed was Luther that two years later, on October 31, 1517, he nailed onto the door of the church in Wittenberg ninety-five statements of protest against his previous system's religious dogma. The resulting firestorm of debate shook the religious world, became known to historians as the Protestant Reformation and redesigned the religious landscape so dramatically that the results are still clearly evident today.

Can you relate to Luther's fear and guilt before God? Can you identify with feeling terrified by the thought of meeting your Creator? Jesus said that he came to set men and women free from the tyranny of religious guilt and fear.

FREEDOM FROM RELIGIOUS WORKS

Do you know the name John Wesley? If you have spent much time in the Methodist Church, I bet you do. Wesley was the founder of Methodism and is credited with helping spark the spiritual awakening that swept through Europe and America in the mid- to late-1700s.

If Martin Luther's religious handicap was guilt, John Wesley's was performance. Wesley was the fifteenth of nineteen children born to two very strict religious parents. Wesley's father was a priest in the Anglican Church and his mother, Susanna, was the daughter of a pastor in London. Wesley cut his spiritual teeth in a religious system that stressed heavy doses of daily prayer and personal Bible study, frequent participation in Holy Communion and had as its goal the "perfection" of the Christian life. He grew up not only learning how to chronicle his spiritual failures but also knowing what rules to keep in order to overcome them.

At age seventeen Wesley entered Oxford and eventually began to prepare for ministry in the Anglican Church. In the mid-1730s, Wesley, along with his brother, Charles, accepted an invitation to serve as an Anglican missionary to the native Indians in the British colony of Georgia.

To say that his time in Georgia was disastrous would be an understatement. Wesley found that he hated the "savage" Indians and that the white colonists he was trying to lead equally disliked him. They resented his strict and rigorous religious practices. To make matters worse, Wesley had an affair with the eighteen-year-old niece of the local Savannah magistrate. The young woman eventually eloped with Wesley's rival, causing him to ban them both from Holy Communion. The couple sued Wesley for slander and the trial actually dragged on for six months. Finally, Wesley had to flee the colony in disgrace.

The long ship ride home gave Wesley a chance to consider the events in Georgia. He wrote, "I went to America to convert the Indians, but, oh, who will convert me?"[19]

John Wesley, Anglican priest and missionary to the American Indians, arrived back in England in a cloud of despair and confusion on February 1, 1738. For twelve years he had labored to arrive at the spiritual perfection that he believed was necessary, only to find himself worn out and beaten by the very religious system that he had served. Then, on May 24, 1738, Wesley reluctantly agreed to attend a church society meeting in Aldersgate. The group was, ironically enough, studying Martin Luther's commentary on Romans, written nearly two hundred years earlier.

Wesley recorded in his journal what happened: "About a quarter to nine, while [the teacher] was describing the change which God works in the heart through faith in Christ, I felt my heart strangely warmed. I felt that I did trust in Christ, Christ alone, for salvation; and an assurance was given me that he had taken away my sins, even mine, and saved me from the law of sin and death."[20]

What Wesley had been unable to accomplish through religious effort was freely offered to him by the gracious hand of God. The resulting change in Wesley led to over forty years of unparalleled ministry and travel where he boldly proclaimed the freedom of grace in Jesus. Before his death in 1774, Wesley logged the equivalent of ten times around the world—over two hundred fifty thousand miles—on horseback—in his efforts to spread the message of the faith in Christ that had so altered his life.

Can you relate to John Wesley's spiritual exhaustion and failure? Have you felt as if you were running on a never-ending treadmill of religious performance? Does it seem as if the religious systems of today are designed more to enslave, rather than liberate, tired souls? If so, then you are in good historical company and you are a prime candidate for the ambush of grace that both Luther and Wesley encountered. Perhaps, just perhaps, when Jesus talked about the truth that sets free, he was talking about his truth that would free *you*, not just from the guilt of your own sin but also from your own futile religious efforts to be rid of it.

AN UNLIKELY CONVERT

Before we conclude this chapter on religion, I would like to offer you one more factual account. This is yet another story of a man who moved from "religion" to Christianity, but his is a bit different. This man had given up on true religion all together. He had bailed on the hope that any faith-based system would ever have room for him. His religion was the pursuit of happiness. His church was the party. His sacrament was anything that satisfied his flesh and dulled his pain. He was his own god, high priest and disciple all rolled up into one. And he was just the kind of person that Jesus said he came to earth to save.

I met Larry Broussard not long after his thirty-eighth birthday. He had only been a Christ-follower for a few weeks. He was also a former homosexual, a recovering alcohol and cocaine addict and HIV positive. I was twenty-five years old at the time and was the pastor of a small Baptist church in north Austin. When

I reached for my seminary text explaining how to connect "people like Larry" with "people like Baptists," I found my bookshelf empty. The year was 1987, and the AIDS virus was still a mystery to many. Doctors were not quite sure how the virus was or was not transmitted. As a result, much fear and confusion still hovered around any discussion of the disease.

The church I served was a sweet and relatively healthy Southern Baptist congregation. We prided ourselves on being welcoming to all and open-minded about the new challenges that God would bring us. However, the idea of a formerly gay guy with AIDS working in the nursery, cooking in the kitchen or serving as a sponsor at youth camp...well let's just say it stretched the limits of open-mindedness for some of our more conservative members.

In my efforts to guide him safely into the fellowship of our church without either of us being lynched, I got to spend a lot of time with Larry. Larry was one of the most remarkable people I had ever known. I am grateful to God for bringing him into the path of my ministry. He was one of the best things that ever happened to our little church. His story is nothing short of amazing.

Larry was a two-time world-champion ballroom dancer. In the sport of competitive ballroom dance, Larry was an international celebrity. When Larry was thirteen, a minister in the church that he and his parents attended molested him. The encounter left him convinced that not only was he gay, but he also was a religious misfit. As a young teenager, Larry wrote off any chance of ever having a meaningful relationship with God or a church. He threw himself into the sport of dance—an area in which he was naturally gifted—and into the party scene. Both soon came to dominate his life.

In February 1987, Larry and his friends made the trek to New Orleans for their annual Mardi Gras celebration. When you live for the party, Mardi Gras is a required stop on the tour. Larry remembered very little about his first few days in New Orleans. He was drunk and/or high the entire time. He also had numerous sexual encounters with several different men and women, most of whom he did not know. Larry would not have labeled such behavior as extreme; it was just how he lived. He moved from place to place, event to event, party to party, person to person, drug to drug, looking to meet the needs of his soul. Larry was a seeker; he just wasn't sure what he was seeking. He had, however, ruled out God as a possibility.

On one of the final nights of Mardi Gras, Larry and some of his friends were out looking for action on Bourbon Street. Larry saw a group of people walking their direction on the other side of the street. He immediately knew that they were not your typical Mardi Gras revelers. Larry quickly identified them as a group of Christians, the kind notorious for roaming the streets of the French Quarter, preaching Hell and judgment and basically trying to ruin everyone else's fun. He could tell they were Christians because they were singing hymns, carrying Bibles and were led by some guy carrying a cross.

Larry snapped. He had been the object of more abuse and ridicule at the hands of "Christians" than he cared to remember. He felt that this group was somehow hostile toward him personally and invading his space. Larry left his friends and boldly marched across the street to confront the would-be evangelists. He verbally lashed out at them for their judgmental attitudes and hypocrisy. He used every derogatory word he knew to vent the pain and humiliation he had felt toward the church for over two decades. But he did not get the fight he expected. Larry's group of Christians seemed, if anything, almost empathetic.

Larry's encounter with the group (who by the way were part of a mission group from a church in Chillicothe, Missouri) lasted over three hours. It ended with Larry kneeling on Bourbon Street, in the midst of a wild Mardi Gras celebration, asking Jesus to forgive his sins and to come into his tattered life. Larry showed up in my church office a month later. He was baptized and warmly received into our fellowship.

A year later, Larry's AIDS kicked in. He was diagnosed with lymphoma, a nasty side effect of having no immune system. Larry literally began to deteriorate before our eyes. Once strong and robust, Larry became frail and weak. His hair fell out from the chemo he was receiving. He was sick almost all of the time, either from the intense treatments or from the lymphoma. Our church cared for Larry and several members nursed him as if he were part of their family. But it was breaking our hearts to watch Larry die.

During that time, Larry never got angry with God over his disease. He was not a victim. Larry knew that he was reaping the consequences of choices he had made in his life before Christ. He was, if anything, thankful for the chance to live out his final days in Christian community. I will never forget the day that I was called to Seton hospital in Austin. Larry was in a coma. To me, he looked dead already and it was difficult to see him that way. I said a prayer over Larry, hugged his grieving parents and then left the bedside of one of the most authentic Christ-followers I had ever known.

And then Larry woke up. And then he got up. And then he went home from the hospital. Larry's lymphoma had "mysteriously" gone into remission. Not only had he not died, but he also had made one of the most amazing comebacks from late-stage lymphoma that his doctors had ever seen. In the next year of

Larry's life, he traveled the world trying to rekindle some of his old friendships from his partying days. He received two lifetime awards from his peers in the ballroom dance community. At both award ceremonies, Larry told the story of how Jesus had found him on the streets of New Orleans, how Jesus had forgiven his sins and how Jesus had given him "extra time" to tell his friends about God's goodness. He did this with complete abandon.

Larry eventually moved to Houston to be closer to his parents. Up until the time when the AIDS virus finally took his life, Larry was active in his church, where he was the leader of a Bible study for men who were trying to break out of the homosexual lifestyle. When Larry died, he was free from any alcohol or drug use and he was celibate. He had lived that way every day since he had heard about a man who told us the truth, years before, on Bourbon Street.

There is one more detail that makes Larry's story even more astounding. In February 1988, instead of making his annual trek to New Orleans, Larry started a new tradition. He traveled to Chillicothe to celebrate the one-year anniversary of his conversion to Christianity with the people who had introduced him to Jesus. They laughed, cried and prayed together as they remembered that night a year before. During the conversation, one of the group's members asked Larry how he had known they were Christians.

Larry's response was immediate: "It was that guy with the cross. The minute I saw the man with the cross in front of your group, I knew who and what you were. That's what caught my attention—it was that guy carrying that cross."

The group looked stunned. They were dead silent.

Larry asked, "What's the matter? Why are you all looking at me like that?"

Someone from the group responded, "Larry, what are you talking about? You're not making any sense. We didn't have any crosses. No one in our group was carrying a cross."

Larry pushed back. "You guys must have forgotten. There was someone, one of you, right in the front of your group, carrying a huge cross. I remember thinking how stupid and out of place a cross looked on Bourbon Street. Come on guys; you're starting to freak me out. Don't you remember the guy with the cross?"

Someone answered, "No, we don't. We didn't have anybody with a cross. Maybe there was a man carrying a cross that wasn't part of our group. Maybe you saw him and just came up to us instead."

Larry was starting to feel a little strange. "No, that's not what happened. I'm sure of it. I knew you guys were Christians, because there was a man leading your group who was carrying a cross. I walked right by him to get to you. He was with your group. Look, I know I was high, but I wasn't hallucinating. I saw a man carrying a cross. He was in your group. That's how I knew you were Christians."

A MAN WHO TOLD US THE TRUTH

Jesus said that one of the major differences between religion and Christianity was point of origin. He said that religions always begin with humans, and because of that, they always fail in finding God. Christianity, said Jesus, was different. Its point of origin was God. In the system that Jesus proclaimed, God first went looking for humans. He taught that only when God illumined our hearts were we able to discern our need for him and reach out to take his already outstretched hand.

I don't know what Larry saw that night on Bourbon Street—an angel, a vision or Jesus himself? I do know that whatever Larry saw got him into position to hear about Jesus. I do know that the Jesus Larry heard about was real enough to free him in one miraculous instant from sexual, alcohol and drug addictions. He was real enough to heal decades of pain, rejection and unforgiveness in Larry. He was real enough to give Larry a reason to live that he had never known before.

Larry's story is one of the reasons why I believe that Jesus was the man who told us the truth. Jesus said that Christianity was different because God came looking for us. Larry's story is proof to me that God will go anywhere, at any time, to love and rescue anyone, regardless of the sin. That is why Christianity is not a religion: you don't have to go looking for God; he is already looking for you.

POINTS FOR PONDERING

After reading this chapter, how would you define religion?

Did you grow up in a "religious" household?

Can you relate to any of the frustrations or failures experienced by Martin Luther and John Wesley before they became Christ-followers?

Can you explain the differences between Christianity and religion? Do you understand why Jesus claimed that Christianity was so unique?

What do you think of Larry's story? Can you relate to the pain and rejection that Larry felt? What do you think could bring about such a radical change in a person's life?

What is your opinion today of Jesus Christ?

CHAPTER 9

I Am
(The Truth about Himself)

• • •

CONGRATULATIONS! YOU HAVE ARRIVED AT the final chapter. I applaud you for sticking with me this far. No doubt you have some level of spiritual interest in Jesus or you probably would have tossed this book a long time ago.

In this chapter, I need to draw the proverbial line in the sand and ask you one last time what you believe about Jesus…but not yet. First, we need to look at a few remaining statements that he made. We will touch on what Jesus said specifically about himself. These statements are the most telling of all. They are the most notorious. I am sure you have heard some of them.

But since we are nearing the end of this journey together and since we are at such a critical point in this process, I would like to pause and pray for you. That may seem somewhat strange, but I feel it is necessary. So if you don't mind, please read the prayer below and just consider that I really am there praying it for you right now.

Dear Father, I believe that you are real. I believe that you are good and loving and that you want to be known. I also believe

in your Son, Jesus. I believe that he is the man who told us the truth. I pray now for this reader. Use the words in the following pages, the words spoken by your Son about himself, to show this reader that you are indeed who Jesus said you were. Do a great thing in this reader's life. I pray this in your holy name. Amen.
OK, I feel much better. Let's get started.

THE SLIM VOLUME

In February 1804, President Thomas Jefferson, ever the enlight-ened rationalist, sat down in the White House with two identical copies of the New Testament, a straight-edge razor and a sheaf of octavo-size paper. Over the course of a few nights, he made quick work of cutting and pasting his own bible, a slim volume he called *The Philosophy of Jesus of Nazareth*. After slicing away every passage that suggested Jesus' divine nature, Jefferson had a Jesus who was no more and no less than a good ethical guide.[21]

Besides the statements we have already considered in previous chapters, I can think of about a dozen more that Jefferson would have had to edit out to get Jesus down to a merely philosophical level. The president had to do some serious cutting to remove all of Jesus' claims of divinity. His was a slim volume indeed. What a shame. Those statements that Jefferson struggled with are the very ones that set Jesus apart from the religious crowd. They are the ones that tell us who Jesus thought he was.

President Jefferson failed to see the futility in his own meth-ods: What good is a philosopher if you have to ferret out all his controversial statements to make him believable? Why learn the teachings of a man only after you have selectively removed those that are too controversial? Should Jesus' distasteful, over-the-top comments negate the value of the more palatable ones? The same Jesus who told us to love our neighbors also claimed to have created them. It seems irrational at best to embrace the rather safe teachings of Jesus and somehow overlook those that are really dangerous. Jesus had no intention of keeping things safe. His radical statements deserve our attention, and it is those remaining radical statements that we examine here.

IT'S ALL ABOUT ME!

Rick Warren, the author of the phenomenally best-selling book *The Purpose Driven Life*, may take the prize for the best first sentence ever written in a book. In four simple words—five measly syllables—Warren rocked our self-absorbed culture to its core: "It's not about you."[22] I remember reading those words for the first time and thinking, *Man, this guy's committing literary suicide. What people would want to buy a book that tells them it's not about them?* But Warren struck a nerve, and his *The Purpose Driven Life* left an indelible imprint on our culture, becoming one of the best-selling books in US history. That is an encouraging sign. Millions in our society seem to resonate with the message that there really is more to life than just satisfying "me." The God-centered philosophy that Warren called for played well to a nation of folks who had it all and were still dissatisfied.

But note this: If Jesus had read Warren's first four words, he might have set the book aside immediately. It is not that Jesus would not agree with Warren's *you are not the point* angle, for he certainly would have. No, it is that Jesus would have seen himself as the one historical exception to the rule. In Jesus' mind, it *was* all about him. In Jesus' theology, he *was* the point.

British scholar and pastor John R. W. Stott eloquently explained Jesus' "me-first" mind-set in his classic book, *Basic Christianity*:

> *The most striking feature of the teaching of Jesus is that he was constantly talking about himself. It is true that he spoke much about the fatherhood of God and the kingdom of God. But then he added that he was the Father's "Son," and that he had come to inaugurate the kingdom. Entry into the kingdom depended on men's response to him. He even did not hesitate to call the kingdom of God "my kingdom." This self-centeredness of the teaching of Jesus immediately sets him apart from the other great religious teachers of the world. They were self-effacing. He was self-advancing. They pointed men away from themselves, saying, "That is the truth, so far as I perceive it; follow that." Jesus said, "I am the truth; follow me." The founder of none of the ethnic religions ever dared to say such a thing.*[23]

Doesn't that seem odd? Doesn't it seem strange, almost hypocritical, that one who would so powerfully command his followers to love and defer to others would have such a "look at me" mind-set? How could Jesus get away with such duplicity? Why would Jesus call others to put themselves last while at the same time asking them to put him first?

OK, here is the straight answer: Jesus believed that he was God. The reason that Jesus told others to look to him was because he believed that he was exactly what they needed. He told others to follow him because he believed he knew "a way" that no one else did. He told people to abide in his words because he knew them to be ultimate. He received worship from others because he believed that he had created them. In short, Jesus went around talking about himself, proclaiming his name and calling others to follow him because he believed that he was God.

If you were God, I suppose, then it would seem perfectly normal for you to talk about yourself so that others might understand you better. However, if you were not God, but went around talking as if you were, then not only would it show that you were in need of serious counseling, but it would also show that you were greatly delusional and should not be trusted. Jesus, evidently, felt it completely appropriate to talk at length about himself. He believed that he had information that we desperately needed and that he was the only means by which we could get it.

John has recorded several statements of Jesus about himself that are not mentioned in the other three gospels. They help set John's gospel apart as the most theological and philosophical of the four, and more importantly, they give us even further insight into Jesus' self-identity. These are the statements that Thomas Jefferson would have had to cut out. These are the claims that set Jesus even further apart from the religious crowd. These are the statements that we must consider when giving Jesus his fair day in court. Here are a few:

- *I am the bread of life. He who comes to me will never go hungry, and he who believes in me will never be thirsty.* (John 6:35)
- *I am the light of the world. Whoever follows me will never walk in darkness, but will have the light of life.* (John 8:12)
- *I tell you the truth, I am the gate for the sheep.* (John 10:7)
- *I am the good shepherd. The good shepherd lays down his life for the sheep.* (John 10:11)
- *I am the resurrection and the life. He who believes in me will live, even though he dies.* (John 11:25)

- *But I, when I am lifted up from the earth, will draw all men to myself.* (John 12:32)
- *You call me "Teacher" and "Lord," and rightly so, for that is what I am.* (John 13:13)
- *I am the true vine, and my Father is the gardener.* (John 15:1)
- *I am the vine; you are the branches. If a man remains in me and I in him, he will bear much fruit; apart from me you can do nothing.* (John 15:5)

It is easy for us to miss the significance of these statements to Jesus' Jewish listeners. In each one, Jesus seized upon imagery that was both familiar and important to Hebrew thinkers. He claimed to be the fulfillment, the realization of what they had been promised for centuries. As the bread of life, Jesus said that he was Heaven's ultimate manna. As the light of the world, Jesus claimed to be the light of God that chased away all darkness. As the door for the sheep, Jesus said that he was the only way into God's green pastures. And as the good shepherd, Jesus promised to lay his life down for his sheep.

At the tomb of his friend Lazarus, Jesus promised to be the resurrection and eternal life spoken of by the Hebrew prophets. Jesus referenced Moses' lifting of a bronze serpent in the wilderness—a source of healing from a plague for all who would look at it—when he claimed that if he were to be lifted up from the earth, he would draw all men to himself. Jesus identified with two key Old Testament images—Teacher and Lord—when he affirmed his disciples for using them to describe him. And when he said he was the vine, Jesus drew upon the vineyard imagery of the Old Testament to describe his relationship to God and his followers' relationship to him.

Now here's a random question: Do these sound like ramblings of a lunatic? It's hard to see someone who so eloquently and strategically identified himself with so many Old Testament images as one who needed to be locked up. Jesus certainly does not sound like he was crazy. But when considering the weight and impact of his comments, lunacy, for many, is the most palatable option.

THAT WOULD BE ME

In one memorable conversation with his enemies, Jesus made a statement that clearly took him out of the "just a nice guy" or "religious leader" category. This one was a doozy, and it almost got him killed; actually, it eventually did: "'I tell you the truth,' Jesus answered, 'before Abraham was born, I am!'" (John 8:58).

In the story of the Exodus found in the Old Testament, God revealed himself to Moses in a miraculous burning bush. When Moses asked whom it was that was sending him to Pharaoh on behalf of the captive Hebrews, God answered, "My name is I AM. When they ask who sent you, tell them that you were sent by I AM." He then told Moses, "This is my name forever, the name by which I am to be remembered from generation to generation" (See Exod. 3:13–15).

This was a precious passage to the Hebrews. In it they were taught that God had not forgotten about them or turned a blind eye to their four-hundred-year captivity in Egypt. The mighty, creating God of the universe had revealed himself to Moses and had begun the process of not just delivering the Hebrews but also reclaiming them as his own chosen people. The passage recorded the salvation of their national and religious identity. To the Jews, it did not just *talk* about holy ground; it *was* holy ground. The name I AM became so revered and holy to the Hebrews that it was considered sinful to even speak it. But that is exactly what Jesus did when he applied it to himself.

In the vice-presidential debate of the 1988 presidential election, Republican nominee Senator Dan Quayle made a passing reference to John F. Kennedy and compared himself to the former president and statesman. Senator Lloyd Bentsen, the crusty and seasoned Democratic nominee, took offense at Quayle's comparison. It led to a classic comment from the Democratic Senator from Texas. He said, "I knew Jack Kennedy. He was a friend of mine. And you, sir, are no Jack Kennedy." Ouch.

Now fast-forward to the 1996 Republican National Convention. Senator Bob Dole was running against presidential incumbent Bill Clinton. The Republicans knew they had a tough job trying to unseat the popular president, so they pulled out the big guns at the convention. Former two-term President Ronald Reagan gave a keynote address on Dole's behalf. Reagan made a now-famous statement that took a jab at Clinton, poked fun at his own old age and recalled Bentsen's great line from the debate eight years earlier. While commenting on the Democrats' frequent comparisons of Clinton to Thomas Jefferson, Reagan said, "I knew Thomas Jefferson. He was a friend of mine. And you, sir, are no Thomas Jefferson." It was a great moment in speech-writing history. Even the Democrats laughed. Well, most of them.

In this I AM statement, that is exactly what Jesus did. He basically said, *Don't talk to me about how much you know about Abraham and what faithful children of Abraham you are. I knew Abraham. I created him! He rejoiced to see my day. And long before Abraham ever existed, my name was I AM.* But Jesus wasn't trying to be funny. He was dead serious.

Jesus took the unspeakable Old Testament name for God and applied it to himself. Such casual references to God and his holy name were considered blasphemous and punishable by death. Jesus knew this. So why would he cross such an obvious cultural and religious line? Was he trying to push the Jewish leader's buttons? Was he disrespecting the God he claimed to love and serve? Was this a slip of Jesus' tongue that revealed his true spiritual colors? Was he really just another spiritual charlatan? Given the rest of Jesus' ministry and statements, that is hard to swallow. Instead, it appears that Jesus was yet again trying to explain to the Jewish leaders exactly who he claimed to be. Where there might have been doubt or confusion previously, this statement removed it all. Jesus' I AM statement made his sense of his own deity undeniable to his audience. They never forgot it and never forgave him for it. After Jesus said this, the plans to kill him came out of the closet. The Jews' efforts to arrest and crucify Jesus went into full gear.

So what do *you* think? Jesus took the oldest, best-known name for the awesome God of Hebrew history and used it to describe himself. He did so with full knowledge of the implications of such a statement and he did so ready to die to back up his point. What do *you* think he was doing?

THE DEAL-BREAKER

Believe it or not, there is actually one final statement of Jesus that is even more infamous than his I AM claim. Jesus spoke it in a private setting to his disciples, so it did not draw the same initial violent response. It is today, however, clearly the most notorious of Jesus' statements. Many spiritual seekers turn away from considering Jesus because of this statement alone. It is that controversial. I once got into a debate with a group of non-Christians at the famous Hyde Park Speaker's Corner in London. The group was made up of people from all over the world (quite typical for a London crowd). Most of them knew and resented this verse. Here it is:

> *I am the way and the truth and the life. No one comes to the Father except through me.* (John 14:6)

For all of its controversy, the statement is pretty easy to interpret. Maybe that is why it is so scandalous: it is hard to read it any other way. Jesus took three familiar images from the Hebrew scriptures—a road or way, truth and life—and used them as metaphors for himself and his mission. Again, there is no surprise here. By now you are used to Jesus taking Old Testament images or concepts and claiming to be the fulfillment of them. He did so here with three powerful images that every good Jew would recognize.

It is the second half of Jesus' statement that spiritual seekers most oppose: "No one comes to the Father except through me." I have talked with hundreds of people about this verse and I think I can sum up their resistance to Jesus' claim. It goes something like this:

> *How could anyone dare to make such a statement? How could anyone have the nerve to be so exclusive? No one can claim to have a monopoly on God. Even if Jesus were really God, why would he create a system that was by nature destined to make so many fail? If God really is Jesus' father, and if Jesus really is the only way to God and if we read this verse the way Jesus intended, then God seems to be guaranteeing that most in history will never find him. What kind of God would do that? Jesus talked about God's love and his desire to be known, and then he turned around and made a statement like this one. That sounds pretty theologically schizophrenic. Which is it? Either God wants*

us to find him or he doesn't. But if he wanted us to find him, he sure as heck (most seekers use stronger language) wouldn't have chosen some reclusive figure in a tiny country in one thirty-three-year segment of history as the gatekeeper. No way.

And then they will ask the question that bothers them the most: *What about all those people in history who never hear of Jesus? What about people in parts of the world that never see a Bible or meet a Christian? What about them? Are they condemned just because they happened to be born in the wrong time or place? And what about all those really good and moral people who are very sincere in their religions? Are they condemned just because they happen to worship a different expression of God? If Jesus really is the only way to God, then God just burned a whole bunch of people from the outset. God is supposed to be good and fair. Well, condemning someone just because they never had the chance to say a specific name (implied—Jesus) isn't fair. How could a God of love do that?*

Is that a close rendering of how you feel? I bet that even if you have not expressed those views yourself, you probably know someone who has.

I think that we are at the moment of truth in this book. If Jesus really was the man who told us the truth, then we have to deal with this statement. I honestly cannot ask you to believe in Jesus while ignoring the difficult and legitimate questions that are raised in the paragraphs above. If you are to make an informed decision about Jesus, then you need all the pieces of the puzzle before you. And no true puzzle of Jesus can be put together with this piece left out. So let's go there. Let's delve into the implications of this statement and try to answer the questions it raises.

WHAT JESUS WAS NOT SAYING

First, let's begin with the frequent misinterpretations of Jesus' comment. Let's look at what he was *not* saying.

Jesus was not saying that he was one way of many. Nothing in the text itself or in any of Jesus' other similar statements even suggests such an interpretation. There is no room in Jesus' language for multiple paths to God. *Jesus was not saying that he was the way for that particular time.* Some try to argue for a cultural or time-specific application. They suggest that while Jesus was indeed claiming to be the only way to God, he was really saying that he was the only way *at that time.* Proponents of this view argue that this leaves the door open to future and additional routes to God.

Again, however, nothing Jesus said seems to even suggest this seasonal-messiah concept. When considered with Jesus' comments about his future return to earth, we are hard pressed to see even a hint of this interpretation in his thinking.

Jesus was not saying that those who never hear of him are automatically condemned. There is no mention in this verse about the requirement of hearing about Jesus. He was not speaking of the need for people to know specifically about him, although he did in other verses. Jesus was simply stating the nature of his relationship to God and his critical role in securing humanity's route back to him.

In other words, while it is impossible for a person to find his way to God apart from the work that Jesus did, it is entirely possible for him to find God without knowing that it was Jesus who helped him get there. It is possible for Jesus to be the means of access to God for individuals even though they are unaware that he has provided such access. Jesus did speak of condemnation, but it was for those who reject or refuse to believe in him. Being unaware of Jesus and his work does not automatically condemn someone before God.

WHAT JESUS WAS SAYING

Now let's consider what Jesus was saying:

Jesus was saying that he was the only way to God. There is no missing this one. Jesus made it clear that he saw himself as the toll road, the tollbooth and the toll payer on the way to God. He was saying that all of humanity's need to reconnect with God was dependent upon him.

As the toll road, Jesus is the only avenue available to man that grants access to God, and that access is not free. As the tollbooth, Jesus provides the only point of entry on the road to God. There are simply no other points of ingress. As the toll payer, Jesus made the payment that made access to God available. That payment was his sacrificial death.

Jesus was saying that there are no alternative routes to God. The way to Heaven is not accessible by varying paths. Since Jesus claimed to be the toll payer, then those routes that bypass him attempt to reach God with the toll unpaid. And since, at least according to Jesus, the issue of sin has caused irreparable damage to humanity's relationship with God, the toll that Jesus paid is required for access.

Attempting to reach Heaven by another route is in essence the same as trying to gain entry into something illegally. If you wish to enter a sporting event or a concert, you are required to have a ticket or a pass. Those at the door don't care how you got it—if you paid for it or if it was a gift; they just know that access cannot be granted without it. Jesus' death on the cross has made access to God available to all. It has provided the ticket, so to speak, to whomever wants it. With such agonizing sacrifice and willing generosity on God's part, those who would seek to approach Heaven through other means are not likely to receive a favorable response from him. He has made free tickets available to every one of us.

Why should we try to impress him on our own merits? What, quite honestly, can you offer him that could even come close to matching the value of the death of his Son? To even try to do so is to cheapen the sacrifice of Jesus and to mock the free gift that he offers. That which is priceless cannot be bought. It can only be given.

WHAT HAPPENS TO PEOPLE WHO NEVER HEAR ABOUT JESUS?

Now that we have considered what Jesus was and was not saying, let's try to answer the most common question that is asked about his *I am the way* statement. You need to know that this is a question that many Christians wrestle with as well. The idea that God would reject someone merely because he has not heard the right information is more than a little troubling, even to Christ-followers. It seems so unlike the God in whom we believe to condemn others who never had the same opportunity to take his claims into account.

And yet that is what we are taught. Many of us were raised in religious systems that said that people could die and go to Hell simply because of their ignorance. Jesus' *I am the way* statement was used as a proof-text for arguing that not having the opportunity to believe is the same as choosing not to and because of that, all the poor, ignorant and unreached souls of the world were condemned to an eternity apart from God.

I need you to know right now that I do not believe that. I do not believe it, not because of how it sounds or makes God look; I do not believe it because it is unbiblical. When we consider the whole of Jesus' teachings, as well as those of the New Testament, we find that God has indeed provided a means of grace for those who have never had the opportunity to believe in Jesus. Jesus is still the only way to God. It is just that some people end up on the way without being aware that he is the one who created it. Let's get to the question.

SUPPOSE THERE WAS A MAN WHO LIVED HIS ENTIRE LIFE ALONE ON A DESERT ISLAND

History is filled with people who did not or will not ever hear the message of forgiveness through Jesus' death. That certainly includes all of those who lived before him. Some readers of the Hebrew scriptures who predated him may have concluded that someone of Jesus' magnitude would come in the future, but such knowledge served only to create hope, not salvation. The bulk of people in history, however, lived and died with no knowledge that a "savior" would come. Many today still live without any awareness of Jesus, even with the proliferation of biblical information. How are they judged? How does God deal with someone who is not aware that Jesus died to cover his or her sins? How does he judge all the people who lived before Jesus?

Here is a biblical concept that you need to know: *Every person is accountable to God for the level of revelation that he receives.* In other words, just as there are different levels of awareness of God, there are also differing levels of accountability to him. Someone with a high God-awareness has an equally high level of accountability. Those with lower levels of understanding are judged by lesser standards. Now before you go and throw a wild party because you're not accountable, I must tell you that we are all accountable to God. No one is excused; no one is off the hook. Even the minimal level of exposure to God is enough to create full accountability to him.

You see, we all start with the same level of God-awareness. We all begin with the same level of God-exposure, and that level comes from one amazing, undeniable and universal source: nature. The Bible flatly asserts that sufficient evidence exists in the created world to not only lead us to conclude that God is real but also make us accountable to him. Consider the biblical writer Paul's words in Romans: "What may be known about God is plain to them, because God has made it plain to them. For since the creation of the world God's invisible qualities—his eternal power and divine nature—have been clearly seen, being understood from what has been made, so that men are without excuse" (Rom. 1:19–20). Over a thousand years earlier, the psalmist David expressed similar convictions: "The heavens declare the glory of God; the skies proclaim the work of his hands. Day after day they pour forth speech; night after night they display knowledge. There is no speech or language where their voice is not heard. Their voice goes out into all the earth, their words to the ends of the world" (Ps. 19:1–4).

Here are two biblical writers, separated by a millennia, both asserting that there is enough information about God built into nature to make every man, woman and child accountable for the knowledge of God. Creation speaks a universal language, one that we all can understand. And in that universal language, nature testifies to the undeniable reality of an awesome and holy source.

Every time you witness a sunset, feel a breeze, gaze up at a star-filled night, listen to the vocal abilities of a parakeet, stare across a field of wildflowers or watch an eagle soar over the rim of a mile-high canyon, you are receiving fresh information about God. Every time you hear a dog bark, hold a newborn's tiny hand, watch the astounding flight skills of a butterfly or hummingbird or witness the raw power of a thunderstorm, you are being taught and instructed about God.

Job, a man tested severely by God in the Old Testament, said it this way: "But ask the animals, and they will teach you, or the birds of the air, and they will tell you; or speak to the earth, and it will teach you, or let the fish of the sea inform you. Which of all these does not know that the hand of the Lord has done this? In his hand is the life of every creature and the breath of all mankind" (Job 12:7–10). The natural conclusion a person should reach, based on the sheer grandeur and the complexity of the created world, is that there is an even more awesome and complex creator.

People who never hear of Jesus are judged on how they respond to the level of awareness of God they do have. God does not judge us for what we do not know; he judges us for what we do know. And the Bible teaches that we each have enough awareness of God through the created world to be fully accountable to him. If a person who never hears of Jesus still responds humbly and reverently to the God of creation, if he believes in and trusts in that God, then the forgiveness made possible by Jesus is applied to him. Jesus becomes that person's way to God, even though he never heard of Jesus. If, however, a person does not respond humbly to God, if he rejects the notion of God or fails to see the evidence of the divine in the created realm, or if he exalts himself as his own god, then Jesus' death does not benefit him. He has no way to access God's forgiveness and thus is judged for his sins. And that, my friend, is never a pretty picture.

If a highly moral person practices a particular religion that draws conclusions about God other than what is revealed about him in nature, then that person is still going to be judged. Many religions, while promoting high levels of ethical living, see God as someone who can be impressed or persuaded by our own righteous deeds. They promote a God who in essence owes us salvation because of how we have lived. They see a God who is required to grant us access simply by the nature of our morality.

That is not the God who is revealed in creation. The only appropriate response to the reality of the creating God is to fall on one's face and to plead for mercy, not to try to impress him or negotiate with him.

The Bible teaches that the testimony of God in the created world is more powerful and persuasive than that of any misguided religion, regardless of how well meaning that religion may be. A person who accepts a religion's distorted view of God and how he is to be approached does so over and against the testimony of the very world in which they live. That is why all people are accountable to God—because they have seen his truth in creation. And that is why people who don't humbly seek God's mercy will be judged for their sins—because they have rejected the very revelation of God that has called them to do so.

Because you are reading this book, or if you have ever read the Bible or heard a sermon about Jesus, or if you had a praying grandmother who used to drag you to Sunday school with her, then you need to know that your level of accountability is very high. You have heard of Jesus and his sacrificial death. And because you have heard, you will be held accountable for that knowledge…and so will I.

All of the people who lived in history before Jesus, all of the other nations and people groups that God created and all of the people today who do not know the claims of Christ, each had or will have ample opportunity to discover and humble themselves before their Creator. If they do, then God is more than pleased to apply the holiness and righteousness made available by Jesus to them. Jesus becomes their Savior. Jesus is still their only way to God: his blood covers their sins and purchases their forgiveness, and it does so because they responded appropriately to the revelation of God that they received. God forgives and saves them, without them ever hearing Jesus' name.

I think that is why Jesus could make his *I am the way* statement with such boldness and confidence. There is no doubt that what Jesus proclaimed was exclusive, but it was not unfair. He knew his God to be good, loving and just.

From God's standpoint, we have to deny the obvious to conclude that he does not exist. Only a deceived heart would determine that bowing humbly before the Creator is unnecessary.

Jesus knew that countless numbers of people who either lived before him or lived and died without full knowledge of him would still have eternal life. He knew that he would sacrifice himself for their sins, that he would die in their place and that he would make a way to God for them. He knew that they would be in Heaven even though they had never expressed belief in him. These people had, at some point in their lives, humbled and surrendered themselves before the God they knew to be obvious, and because of that, to quote Genesis, it was "credited to them as righteousness." (See Gen. 15:6.)

When Jesus said that he was the way, the truth and the life, and that no one comes to God but through him, he was telling the truth. As God's holy Son, he made the only acceptable provision to God for sins. If people are to find favor with God, then it must be on his terms. He defined those terms as forgiveness for sin that was applied through the death of Jesus. Not knowing about Jesus' death is not sin, but knowing about it and rejecting it is.

THE MAN WHO TOLD US THE TRUTH

I believe that Jesus was the man who told us the truth. He told us the truth about ourselves—our origins, our needs, our God baggage and our potential. He told us the truth about God—his love for us, his plan for us and his efforts to rescue us from our sins. He told us the truth about evil—its true source, its ability to control us and how he was going to conquer it. He told us the truth about death and Heaven. He taught us that death need not be feared, and he promised that, if we followed him, he would come back and personally take us to Heaven. He told us the truth about love—love that is unmerited and undeserved and love that does not require reciprocity—and commanded us to love each other as he loved us. And finally, he told us the truth about himself. He claimed to be a man who told us exactly what he heard from God. He claimed to be one with the creating God of the universe. He said that he had come to save us, that he would rise from the dead (an event that remains irrefutable in history), that he would send us his Holy Spirit to guide us and that he would come back to establish his kingdom on earth. He talked to God as if he were a peer; he accepted worship and claimed to be both Teacher and Lord. He said that if he was lifted up from the earth, he would draw all people to himself.

I wonder if he is drawing you now?

What Do You Do Now?

Do you believe that Jesus was the man who told us the truth? Do you believe what he claims about himself? Do you believe what he said about God? I am not asking if you know these things; I am asking if you believe them. Belief is all that is required.

If you believe, then I invite you to embrace him today. It is not difficult to do. For such a radical, life-changing act, it is really quite simple. In fact, you are probably 99 percent there already.

Jesus said, "I tell you the truth, whoever hears my word and believes him who sent me has eternal life and will not be condemned; he has crossed over from death to life" (John 5:24). I like to refer to embracing Jesus and his claims as "crossing the line," for that is really what you are doing. When you accept Jesus as the man who told us the truth, you are crossing the line from unbelief to belief. When you accept him, you cross the line from seeker to follower. When you accept him, you cross the line from unforgiveness and condemnation to forgiveness and grace. And, when you embrace Jesus, you cross the line from death to life.

God does not expect you to be perfect or sinless. He does not expect you to understand it all and have all the answers. But he does expect you to act on what you believe. So cross the line. Get down on your knees, turn your hands over, palms up, and confess your belief in Jesus. Acknowledge your own sin and need for him. Thank him for dying for you. Invite him into your life and declare yourself his forgiven follower. It will be a moment you will never forget.

Then, get up from your knees and do two more things. First, go to church this week, and then keep visiting churches until you find one that feels like home. Remember, there is no such thing as a perfect church, so don't look for one. Second, get a Bible and start reading it. I recommend either the *New International Version* or the *English Standard Version*. Both are good, accurate and unbiased translations of the Hebrew and Greek texts of the Bible. Start reading in Matthew, Mark, Luke or John in the New Testament. These are the four biblical accounts of Jesus' life, and they will remind you of what you have read and expand upon what you have already learned about Jesus.

If you are not there yet, if you are not ready to declare belief and faith in Jesus, I encourage you to keep reading about him. Answers to your questions are out there; but remember, at some point you will still have to proceed in your pursuit of God based on your faith, not just your knowledge. Other books I recommend about Jesus are:

Letters from a Skeptic, by Greg Boyd
Basic Christianity, by John R.W. Stott
Mere Christianity, by C. S. Lewis
The Case for Christ, by Lee Strobel
The Case for Faith, by Lee Strobel
More Than a Carpenter, by Josh McDowell

YOUR FINEST HOUR

When Jesus was hanging on the cross, suspended between heaven and earth, it was his finest hour. In that hour, he showed his love not only for his Father through his rugged obedience but also for you. He showed that you mattered to him, enough that he should die for you. He demonstrated that you were worth pursuing, worth wooing and worth the sacrifice of his life. He showed that the religious systems of humans were not good enough for your spirit. He showed that your soul could only be redeemed by something of greater value—him.

When Jesus died, he dealt once and for all with the issue that separated you from God and threatened to condemn you in eternity. When he died, he paved the way to God for you by his own blood. When Jesus died, he proved that he was not a great religious leader, but rather the greatest religious offering. And when he died, he left the door open for you to become part of the largest and most blessed family in the world—God's. Jesus did all of this for you when he died.

When Jesus died for you, it was his finest hour. When you embrace him, it will be yours.

N O T E S

1 *Merriam-Webster Online (Merriam-Webster's Collegiate Dictionary, Eleventh Edition)*, s.v. "truth," accessed December 27, 2015, http://www.merriam-webster.com/dictionary/truth.

2 Anita Hamilton, "All the Right Questions," *Time*, April 5, 2004, 65.

3 Unless otherwise noted, all scripture quotations are from *New International Version* (NIV) Copyright 1973, 1978, 1984, 2011 by Biblica, Inc. Used by permission. All rights reserved worldwide.

4 Patricia Sellers, *Fortune*, May 26, 2003, 130.

5 Jeremiah Creedon, "God with a Million Faces," *UTNE Reader*, August 1998, 45.

6 Frank McCourt, "When You Think of God What Do You See?" *Life*, December 1998, 63.

7 Lance Armstrong, *It's Not about the Bike* (New York, NY: Berkley Books, 2001), 17.

8 Ibid., 20.

9 Ibid., 116–117.

10 Ron Rosenbaum, "The End of Evil?" *The Spectator*, September 30, 2011, http://www.slate.com/articles/health_and_science/the_spectator/2011/09/does_evil_exist_neuroscientists_say_no_.html

11 Kenneth Woodward, "Do We Need Satan?" *Newsweek*, November 12, 1995, http://www.newsweek.com/do-we-need-satan-181030.

12 Edward Boyd and Gregory Boyd, *Letters from a Skeptic.* (Colorado Springs, CO: Life Journey, 2003), 17–18.

13 Martin Luther King Jr., *Stride Toward Freedom.* (San Francisco, CA: Harper & Row, 1986), 104–105.

14 David Van Biema, "Does Heaven Exist?" *Time*, March 24, 1997, 72.

15 Ibid., 72–73.

16 C. S. Lewis, *The Problem of Pain*, quoted in *The Quotable C. S. Lewis*, Wayne Martindale and Jerry Root, eds. (Wheaton, IL: Tyndale House Publishers, 1989), 281–282.

17 Lawrence M. Small, "Lighthouse of the Skies," *Smithsonian*, July 2003, 10.

18 Bruce Shelly, *Church History in Plain Language.* (Waco, TX: Word Books), 257.

19 Ibid., 354.

20 Ibid., 355.

21 Linda Kulman and Jay Tolson, "Jesus in America," *US News and World Report*, December 22, 2003, 45.

22 Rick Warren, *The Purpose Driven Life* (Grand Rapids, MI: Zondervan, 2002), 17.

23 John R. W. Stott, *Basic Christianity* (Grand Rapids, MI: William B. Eerdmans, 1971), 23.

Made in United States
North Haven, CT
28 November 2021